JUN 1 1 2003

Mountain Biking
Spokane–Coeur d'Alene

SECOND EDITION

NO LONGER PROPERTY OF
SEATTLE PUBLIC LIBRARY

D0052250

Help Us Keep This Guide Up to Date

Every effort has been made by the authors and editors to make this guide as accurate and useful as possible. However, many things can change after a guide is published—establishments close, phone numbers change, hiking trails are rerouted, facilities come under new management, etc.

We would love to hear from you concerning your experiences with this guide and how you feel it could be made better and be kept up to date. While we may not be able to respond to all comments and suggestions, we'll take them to heart and we'll also make certain to share them with the authors. Please send your comments and suggestions to the following address:

The Globe Pequot Press
Reader Response/Editorial Department
P.O. Box 480
Guilford, CT 06437

Or you may e-mail us at:

editorial@globe-pequot.com

Thanks for your input, and happy travels!

A **FALCON** GUIDE ®

Mountain Biking
Spokane–Coeur d'Alene

SECOND EDITION

MARTIN POTUCEK

FALCON®

GUILFORD, CONNECTICUT
HELENA, MONTANA

AN IMPRINT OF THE GLOBE PEQUOT PRESS

Copyright © 2003 by The Globe Pequot Press
A previous edition was published by Falcon Publishing, Inc., in 1999

All rights reserved. No part of this book may be reproduced or transmitted
in any form by any means, electronic or mechanical, including photocopy-
ing and recording, or by any information storage and retrieval system, except
as may be expressly permitted by the 1976 Copyright Act or by the pub-
lisher. Requests for permission should be made in writing to The Globe
Pequot Press, P.O. Box 480, Guilford, Connecticut 06437.

Falcon and FalconGuide are registered trademarks of The Globe Pequot
Press.

ISBN 0-7627-2692-X

Manufactured in the United States of America
Second Edition/First Printing

The Globe Pequot Press assumes no liability for accidents happening
to, or injuries sustained by, readers who engage in activities described in
this book.

Contents

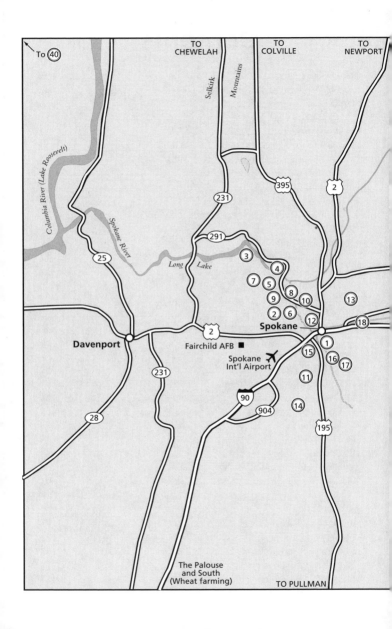

TO CHEWELAH

TO COLVILLE

TO NEWPORT

To 40

Selkirk Mountains

Columbia River (Lake Roosevelt)

Spokane River

231

395

2

291

25

Long Lake

3

4

7

5

8

9

10

2

6

13

12

18

Spokane

Davenport

2

Fairchild AFB

Spokane Int'l Airport

1

15

16

17

231

11

90

904

14

28

195

The Palouse and South (Wheat farming)

TO PULLMAN

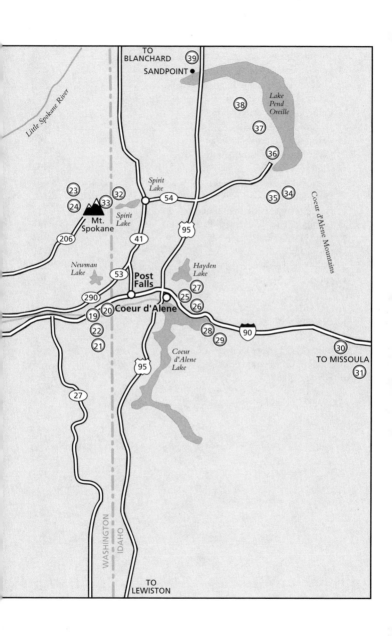

Idaho and Vicinity

Farther Afield

Acknowledgments

This book represents more than a thousand miles in the saddle, spread over sixty days, but that is only the time and distance I have put in. A wide range of people—some of whom I am close to and some others whom I have not even met yet—pedaled many more miles and contributed time, energy, and insights. This section is mostly a thanks to all the good folks in the Spokane-Idaho Panhandle area who were so helpful and willing to share some of their territory and perhaps some of their secrets.

This is not to say I have unearthed the vast system of trails and roads that crisscross this land. Although the written history goes back little more than a century, it tells of wild times in both natural and "civilized" realms. Part of that history is left in the earth that was surveyed, logged, mined, railroaded, paved, and delivered to us in the present state. There are packsaddle trails, winding steeper than any bike can climb; there are wagon or light rail tracks that have never been used beyond the occasional skidder or rocket sled. In these pages is but a sampling of the routes that are out there; surprisingly, a lot of them are still legally accessible.

Consider, too, that these offerings are not always the most elegant or even the best choice for a certain area, but they all strive to be representative and a good introduction to an area. Once the rider finds a new spot, a process of investigation and variation sets in, and intimacy comes only after time. That's especially true of areas like Riverside State Park or Canfield Mountain, where the trails are complex systems and the choices are many.

My brothers-in-law Kelly Greenwood and Russ VanderWilde have to share some of the credit for showing me their hidden neighborhoods. A highlight occurred when

Kelly took me through a forested archery range just before bow season.

Kasey Kramer showed me Marshall, High Drive, and the finer points of duct-taping your Achilles tendon. Tim Kincaid showed me how to appreciate lunch at the old Kirk's Lodge after pedaling Mount Spokane all day.

Mark Beattie at Vertical Earth in Coeur d'Alene amazes me that he can sell and fix all those gravity machines and still find time and energy to push his butt up the hill.

Margaret Watson, with the Spokane Bicycle Club, connected me to Clyde Anderson, whom I just happened to bump into on the Centennial Trail the next day. Clyde was a wealth of information concerning local biking issues.

Tom Mosher and the Spokane Mountaineers were excellent sources of information and feedback and helped me figure out some subtleties surrounding Browne's Mountain and lower High Drive.

Gary Herron, of Riverside State Park, was warm and generous with his knowledge and seemed to have a true appreciation for the special piece of earth that he manages.

Dick Snyder, of Inland Empire Paper Co., was also one of the land stewards who gave me advice and directions. The holdings of IEP are strategic for recreationalists of all kinds, and, were it not for their benign stewardship practices and open-door policies, outdoors enthusiasts' options would be greatly diminished; consider the Nordic trails at Mount Spokane.

Judy York at the Sandpoint Ranger District Office was friendly and forthcoming with what trail information she had. National Forest land as a whole probably represents the largest single chunk of trail potential in this country, but managers of public lands such as these do not have the autonomy of management options a private sector counterpart might. Other forest service people who helped were Mike Almas in Kettle Falls, Washington, and Andy Boggs at the Fernan District in Coeur d'Alene. And a special thanks to Sam(antha) at Fernan and Silver Mountain who energized me with her enthusiasm for the potential of the Silver Valley's surrounding peaks.

Mike Aho and Paul Crutchfield of the Spokane City Parks and Recreation Department were great sources of insight into the complexities of management plans and conflicting interests in the burgeoning city. Mike was especially helpful with on-site editing, sometimes at 20 mph with me bouncing along behind, voice recording in my best one-handed technique. Wyn Berkenthal of the Spokane County Parks Department heightened my awareness for the importance of discretion, especially when dealing with private-public land issues. Bryant, who helps manage Spokane County's Liberty Lake Park, was also highly enthusiastic and helpful. The news is mostly good for area enthusiasts: We are endowed with progressive, caring stewards who themselves are known to pedal or jog a mile or two.

Dara at Silver Mountain and Sherry at Snowblaze on Mount Spokane I want to thank for their helpfulness with information, water, and a lift.

John McCreedy was instrumental in ferreting out the legal parameters of trespass and public domain in Washington and Idaho, and in this day and age, we may even need to know about the six-inch log's ability to float down a stream during a hundred-year flood.

And finally, thanks to my main team: Trish, Bryce, Connor, and Alizabeth, who will never let me go back to being a load in the shorts again.

Locator Map for USGS 7.5-minute Topos

Legend

～ Singletrack		START ⓪	Trailhead	
～ Doubletrack		X	Elevation/Peak	
～ Improved Road		🛡90	Interstate	
～ Interstate		②2	U.S. Highway	
⌐ Wilderness/Park Boundary		㊼54	State Highway/County Road	
～ Waterway		2030	Forest Road	
～ Intermittent Waterway		⊶	Gate	
Lake/Reservoir		■	Building	
⚜ Wetlands		⌣	Pass/Saddle	
╱╱╱ Cliff		⊢⊢⊢⊢	Railroad	
△ Camping		⋈	Bridge/Trestle	
ⓟ Parking		✗	Mine Site	
N Scale/Compass		⊙	Radio Tower	
		•—•—•	Power Line	
0 0.5 1		▦	Urban Area	
MILES			Gas Pipeline	
		⊐▯⊏	Tunnel	

Get Ready to Crank!

Welcome to *Mountain Biking Spokane–Coeur d'Alene*. Here are forty rides ranging from easy road routes to subalpine technical ascents. The rides are described in plain language, with accurate distances and ratings for physical and technical difficulty. Each entry offers detailed information that's easy to read and use, from armchair or trailside. A glossary of terms is included at the end of the book.

Whether you're a local sprockethead, an intermediate wanting to improve your range and skill, or just someone looking for an easier or different ride, this book is for you.

Our aim is multifold: to help you choose a ride that's appropriate for your fitness and skill level; to make it easy to find the trailhead; to help you complete the ride safely, without getting lost; and, of course, maybe even to introduce you to new territory.

All of the rides in this guide are located in or near Spokane or Coeur d'Alene. All can be started and finished by bike, although the more outlying rides, like Columbia Mountain or those in the Sandpoint area, can be reached by driving. Rides are presented as loops, beginning and ending at the same point.

The information given in this guide should be considered a basic tool for your mountain biking adventures, benefiting from the experience (mistakes) of others. This book operates on this ethic: that with these tools (this knowledge) comes the responsibility to travel safely and prudently, and to respect the rights of others, whether they're landowners, loggers, or lizards.

Whether the boundaries of the group are definable or not, there is a community in the Inland Northwest that shares the same urges: to discover and travel the terrain lightly and quickly, and without leaving a trace. There has been a huge wave of support for pushing the Centennial Trail from Coeur d'Alene to Nine Mile (northwest of Spokane), connecting bikers through a single ribbon of dedicated asphalt, allowing you to traverse the entire metropolitan area with your muscles, safely. Please consider that when you venture out, you are a model, an ambassador, who helps write the future policies for this area.

Note to the Second Edition

Heavily used areas around Spokane have seen a substantial amount of trail building since the first edition of this guidebook. Mostly, this wonderful achievement of human effort was not made through public consensus or process. It was made in the shadows by individuals and small groups one might call recreation activists. They were certainly bikers, although some runners may have lent a hand or two. Whether you condone, applaud, or condemn the radical trail construction of Deep Rut and others of his ilk, you cannot deny that there are simply more trails out there today. Areas like Beacon Hill and High Drive are most noticeable, but as my own experience has led me to believe, that activism is spreading. When you're in these areas, be on the lookout for tracks that weren't there before. It would be impossible to try to catalog these, and in so doing, they would be legitimized. Only time will tell which will remain well traveled and which will go back to the natural state.

The Hangman Park ride was removed from the present edition due to access problems between public lands and private-property owners. This kind of problem is nothing new in the West and won't go away any time soon. Not to bring Idaho values to a progressive place like Spokane, but it's strange that subdivisions are still approved without regard to adjacent public-land access.

A new ride has been added, Hiawatha Rail Trail, Ride 31, due to its widespread popularity.

Another addition to the second edition is an entry in Appendix A, Other Spokane-Area Routes. It's a brief description of the Trail of the Coeur d'Alenes, a paved, nonmotorized pathway from Plummer to Mullan, Idaho, that stretches more than 70 miles. It's one of the nation's most spectacular reclaimed rail trails, passing over or near Coeur d'Alene Lake and River and the St. Joe River (a river within a lake). Road bikers and mountain bikers alike, along with skaters and joggers, will want to check out this new addition to the area's playbook.

The Spokane–Coeur d'Alene Area: What to Expect

The rides in this book cover a wide variety of terrain—from Riverside State Park, where rocky loops span the full technical spectrum, to loops like Beauty Creek–Caribou Ridge, rising thousands of feet over pavement and logging roads, only to dive down a steep, highly technical precipice. Not all the areas are for everyone, but there is something for everyone.

Although Spokane and the lower valley are a bit milder and warmer than their surroundings, consider this whole area (roughly a 60-mile radius) to be northern temperate. This means it gets cold, with big storms that leave snow and ice on the ground in winter. Consider, too, that cougar, bear, and moose have been spotted and trapped in the city, mostly in areas where the urban rides are described. So watch out, and be aware of all the deadly and dangerous things that can happen to you out there. Some of the terrain described is ridable only about three months a year.

Mountain terrain requires preparedness. Know your equipment, and know your abilities. This book is not intended as a primer or guide to the sport of mountain biking; it's a guide to specific rides with specific conditions *that are changing constantly.* Those starting out should try the shorter, easier routes, and then, as conditioning and skill improve, reach for the longer, more difficult rides. Take your time; enjoy your rides, even your workouts. Injuries are likely to occur with speed or fatigue; I advocate always maintaining a little energy reserve to get you out of trouble.

Whatever your motivation for biking is, this book is written with the following premise: that it's noncompetitive and nonegocentric; the thrill of the experience lies between the terrain and you. All else is distraction and window dressing; it doesn't matter what generation Lycra you wear or whether you're fully suspended. When pumping a sustained steep hill or preparing to launch some precipice, chill your jets for a moment—take a look around.

At any time of year, rain or snow can turn trails to puree for days afterward. Please stay off wet, muddy trails. The risk of soil damage and erosion is simply too great. A good rule of thumb: If you leave a track, don't go. Conversely, in midsummer trails tend to dry out—are less compacted and sandier—and thus are more difficult to climb in the steeper sections.

"Posted: No Trespassing"

The greater Spokane area is fortunate to have a number of mountain ranges within a two-hour drive, and within one hour more rides than you could do in a year. Spanning two states, Washington and Idaho, is a wide array of public and private lands, many that are open to public use, but some are not. See Appendix B for a partial listing of land management agencies in the area.

Familiarize yourself with your state's trespass laws: Idaho Code, sections 18-7008, 18-7011, 6-202, 6-202A, and 5-218. Washington's can be found under 9A.52.070, 9A.52.080, 9A.52.090, and 79.01.760 of the Revised Code of Washington Annotated.

In general, a person can be found guilty of criminal trespass if he or she knowingly enters or remains unlawfully on another person's property. If property is posted against trespass, no one is allowed to enter without explicit permission from the landowner. Your best protection is to always obtain express permission to ride on private property.

Rules of the Trail

If every mountain biker always yielded the right-of-way, stayed on the trail, avoided wet or muddy trails, never cut switchbacks, never skidded, always rode in control, showed respect for other trail users, and carried out every last scrap of what was carried in (candy wrappers and bike-part debris included)—in short, did the right thing—then we wouldn't need a list of rules governing our behavior.

Fact is, most mountain bikers are conscientious and are trying to do the right thing. Most of us *own* that integrity.

Here are some guidelines, reprinted by permission from the International Mountain Bicycling Association (IMBA). The basic theme here is to reduce or eliminate any damage to the land and water, the plant and wildlife inhabitants, and other backcountry visitors and trail users—to ride with respect.

IMBA Rules of the Trail

1. Ride on open trails only. Respect trail and road closures (ask if not sure), avoid possible trespass on private land, obtain permits and authorization as may be required. Federal and state wilderness areas are closed to cycling. The way you ride will influence trail management decisions and policies.

2. Leave no evidence. Be sensitive to the dirt beneath you. Even on open (legal) trails, you should not ride under conditions where you will leave evidence of your passing, such as on certain soils after a rain. Recognize different types of soil and trail construction; practice low-impact cycling. This also means staying on existing trails and not creating any new ones. Be sure to pack out at least as much as you pack in.

3. Control your bicycle! Inattention for even a second can cause problems. Obey all bicycle speed regulations and recommendations.

4. Always yield trail. Make known your approach well in advance. A friendly greeting (or bell) is considerate and works well; don't startle others. Show your respect when passing by, slowing to a walking pace or even stopping. Anticipate other trail users around corners or in blind spots.

5. Never spook animals. All animals are startled by an unannounced approach, a sudden movement, or a loud noise. This can be dangerous for you, others, and the animals. Give animals extra room and time to adjust to you. When passing horses, use special care and follow directions from the horseback riders (ask if uncertain). Running cattle and disturbing wildlife is a serious offense. Leave gates as you found them, or as marked.

6. Plan ahead. Know your equipment, your ability, and the area in which you are riding—and prepare accordingly. Be self-sufficient at all times, keep your equipment in good repair, and carry necessary supplies for changes in weather or other conditions. A well-executed trip is a satisfaction to you and not a burden or offense to others. Always wear a helmet.

Keep trails open by setting a good example of environmentally sound and socially responsible off-road cycling.

How to Use This Guide

Mountain Biking Spokane–Coeur d'Alene describes forty mountain bike rides in their entirety. A handful of other local routes are mentioned briefly in Appendix A.

Most of the featured rides are loops, beginning and ending at the same point but following a different route on the return. Some rides in this guide are out-and-backs, coming and going the same route; this is avoided where possible.

Be forewarned, however: The difficulty of a loop ride may change dramatically depending on which direction you ride. If you are unfamiliar with the rides in this book, try them first as described here. The directions follow the path of least resistance (which does not necessarily mean "easy"). After you've been over the terrain, you can determine whether a given loop would be fun—or even feasible—in the reverse direction.

Portions of some rides follow gravel and even paved roads, and a handful of rides never wander off-road. Purists may wince at road rides in a book about mountain biking, but these are special rides. They offer a chance to enjoy the scenery and fresh air while covering easier, nontechnical terrain—good for people new to the sport. They can also be used by hard-core riders on "active rest" days or when higher elevation trails are closed by mud or snow.

Each ride description follows the same format:

Number and name of the ride: Rides are cross-referenced by number throughout this book. In many cases, parts of rides or entire routes can be linked to other rides for longer trips or variations of a standard route.

For the names of rides, I relied on official names of trails, roads, and natural features as shown on National Forest and U.S. Geological Survey maps.

Location: The general whereabouts of the ride; distance and direction from Spokane/Coeur d'Alene.

Distance: The length of the ride in miles, given as a loop or round-trip.

Time: An estimate of how long it takes to complete the ride, for example: 1 to 2 hours. The time listed is the actual riding time and does not include rest stops. Strong, skilled riders may be able to do a given ride in less than the estimated time, while other riders may take considerably longer. Also, severe weather, changing trail conditions, or mechanical problems may prolong a ride.

Tread: The type of road or trail: paved road, gravel road, dirt road or jeep track, doubletrack, and singletrack.

Aerobic level: The level of physical effort required to complete the ride: easy, moderate, or strenuous (see the explanation of the rating systems on page 12).

Technical difficulty: The level of bike-handling skills needed to complete the ride upright and in one piece. Technical difficulty is rated on a scale from 1 to 5, with 1 being the easiest and 5 the hardest (see the explanation of the rating systems on page 13).

Hazards: A list of dangers that may be encountered on a ride, including traffic, weather, trail obstacles and conditions, risky stream crossings, difficult route finding, and other perils. Remember: Conditions may change at any time. Be alert for storms, new fences, downfall, missing trail signs, and mechanical failure. Fatigue, heat, cold, and/or dehydration may impair judgment. Always wear a helmet and other safety equipment. Ride in control at all times.

Highlights: Special features or qualities that make a ride worth doing: scenery, fun singletrack, chances to see wildlife.

Land status: A list of managing agencies and private inholdings. Most of the rides in this book are on National Forest, state park, or Bureau of Land Management lands. But many of the rides also cross portions of private or municipal lands. Always leave gates as you found them. Respect the land, regardless of who owns it. See Appendix B for a list of local addresses for land-managing agencies.

Maps: A list of available maps. National Forest and local publications (parks, recreation areas, etc.) are listed, where pertinent. USGS topographic maps in the 7.5-minute quad series provide a close-up look at terrain. Also, the Bureau of Land Management 1:100,000 map for Spokane shows topography and many travel routes for the area. Not all routes are shown on official maps.

Access: How to find the trailhead or the start of the ride. Most rides can be pedaled right from town; for others it's best to drive to the trailhead.

The ride: A mile-by-mile list of key points—landmarks, notable climbs and descents, stream crossings, obstacles, hazards, major turns and junctions—along the ride. All distances were measured to the tenth of a mile with a cyclometer (a bike-mounted odometer). Terrain, riding technique, and even tire pressure can affect odometer readings, so treat all mileages as estimates.

Finally, one last reminder that the real world is changing all the time. The information presented here is as accurate and up-to-date as possible, but there are no guarantees out there. You alone are responsible for your safety and for the choices you make on the trail.

If you do find an error or omission in this book, or a new and noteworthy change in the field, I'd like to hear from you. Please write to Martin Potucek, c/o The Globe Pequot Press, P.O. Box 480, Guilford, Connecticut 06437.

Rating the Rides—One Person's Pain Is Another's Pleasure

Globe Pequot's Falcon mountain biking guides rate each ride for two types of difficulty: the physical effort required to pedal the distance and the level of bike-handling skills needed to stay upright and make it home in one piece. We call these "Aerobic level" and "Technical difficulty."

The following sections explain what the various ratings mean in plain, specific language. An elevation profile accompanies each ride description to help you determine how easy or hard the ride is. Also weigh other factors such as elevation above sea level, total trip distance, weather and wind, and current trail conditions.

Aerobic Level Ratings

Bicycling is often touted as a relaxing, low-impact, relatively easy way to burn excess calories and maintain a healthy heart and lungs. Mountain biking, however, tends to pack a little more work (and excitement) into the routine.

Fat tires and soft or rough trails increase the rolling resistance, so it takes more effort to push those wheels around. Unpaved or off-road hills tend to be steeper than grades measured and surfaced by the highway department. When we use the word *steep,* we mean a sweat-inducing, oxygen-sucking, lactose-building climb. If it's followed by an exclamation point—steep (!)—expect some honest pain on the way up (and maybe for days afterward).

So expect to breathe hard and sweat some, probably a lot. Pedaling around town is a good start, but it won't fully prepare you for the workout offered by most of the rides in this book. If you're unsure of your level of fitness, see a doctor for a physical exam before tackling any of the rides in this book. And if you're riding to get back in shape or just for the fun of it, take it easy. Walk or rest if need be. Start with short rides and add on miles gradually.

Here's how we rate the exertion level for terrain covered in this book:

Easy: Flat or gently rolling terrain. No steeps or prolonged climbs.

Moderate: Some hills. Climbs may be short and fairly steep or long and gradual.

Strenuous: Frequent or prolonged climbs steep enough to require riding in the lowest gear; requires a high level of aerobic fitness, power, and endurance (typically acquired through many hours of riding and proper training). Less fit riders may need to walk.

Many rides are mostly easy and moderate but may have short strenuous sections. Other rides are mostly strenuous and should be attempted only after a complete medical checkup and implant of a second heart, preferably a *big* one. Also be aware that flailing through a highly technical section can be exhausting even on the flats. Good riding skills and a relaxed stance on the bike save energy.

Finally, any ride can be strenuous if you ride it hard and fast. Conversely, the pain of a lung-burning climb grows easier to tolerate as your fitness level improves. Learn to pace yourself and remember to schedule easy rides and rest days into your calendar.

Technical Difficulty Ratings

While you're pushing up that steep, strenuous slope, wondering how much farther you can go before collapse, remember that the condition of your heart, lungs, and legs aren't the only factors on the way to the top of the mountain. There's that tree across the trail, or the side slope full of ball-bearing-size pebbles, or the place where the trail fades to a tire smear on a rock face overlooking an abyss.

Mountain bikes will roll over or through an amazing array of challenges, but sometimes we, as riders, have to help. And, even more astonishing, some riders get off their bikes and walk—get this—*before* they flip over the handlebars. Those who lack this kind of humility may later brag about the "ride to hell" (leaving out the part about carrying the bike half the distance because "hell" has some highly technical terrain).

The technical difficulty ratings in this book help take the worst surprises out of backcountry rides. In the privacy of your own home, you can make an honest appraisal of your bike-handling skills and then find rides in these pages that are within your ability.

We rate technical difficulty on a scale from 1 to 5, from easiest to most difficult. We tried to make the ratings as objective as possible by considering the type of obstacles and their frequency of occurrence. The same standards were applied consistently through all the rides in this book.

We've also added plus (+) and minus (-) symbols to cover gray areas between given levels of difficulty: a 4+ obstacle is harder than a 4, but easier than a 5-. A stretch of trail rated as 5+ would be unridable by all but the most skilled (or luckiest) riders.

Here are the 5 levels defined:

Level 1: Smooth tread; road or doubletrack; no obstacles, ruts, or steeps. Requires basic bike-riding skills.

Level 2: Mostly smooth tread; wide, well-groomed single-track or road/doubletrack with minor ruts or loose gravel or sand.

Level 3: Irregular tread with some rough sections; single or doubletrack with obvious route choices; some steep sections; occasional obstacles may include small rocks, roots, water bars, ruts, loose gravel or sand, and sharp turns or broad, open switchbacks.

Level 4: Rough tread with few smooth places; singletrack or rough doubletrack with limited route choices; steep sections, some with obstacles; obstacles are numerous and varied, including rocks, roots, branches, ruts, sidehills, narrow tread, loose gravel or sand, and switchbacks.

Level 5: Continuously broken, rocky, root-infested, or trenched tread; singletrack or extremely rough doubletrack with few route choices; frequent, sudden, and severe changes in gradient; some slopes so steep that wheels lift off ground; obstacles are nearly continuous and may include boulders, logs, water, large holes, deep ruts, ledges, piles of loose gravel, steep sidehills, encroaching trees, and tight switchbacks.

Again, most of the rides in this book cover varied terrain, with an ever-changing degree of technical difficulty. Some trails run smooth with only occasional obstacles, and other trails are seemingly all obstacle. The path of least resistance, or *line,* is where you find it. In general, most obstacles are more challenging if you encounter them while climbing than while descending. On the other hand, in heavy surf (e.g., boulder fields, tangles of downfall, cliffs), fear plays a larger role when facing downhill.

Realize, too, that different riders have different strengths and weaknesses. Some folks can scramble over logs and boulders without a grunt, but they crash head over heels on every switchback turn. Some fly off the steepest drops and others freeze. Some riders climb like the wind and others just blow—and walk.

The key to overcoming "technical difficulties" is practice: keep trying. Follow a rider who makes it look easy, and don't hesitate to ask for constructive criticism. Try shifting your weight (good riders move a lot, front to back, side to side, and up and down), and experiment with balance and momentum. Find a smooth patch of lawn and practice riding as slowly as possible, even balancing at a standstill in a "track stand." This will give you more confidence—and more time to recover or bail out—the next time the trail rears up and bites.

Spokane and Points West

Highbridge–Vinegar Flats Loop

Location: 1 mile west of downtown Spokane, near Latah Creek.

Distance: 4.2-mile loop.

Time: 30 minutes.

Tread: 2.4 miles paved, 1.7 miles dirt/gravel road or railroad bed, 0.1 mile singletrack.

Aerobic level: Easy.

Technical difficulty: 2.

Hazards: Traffic; loose gravel.

Highlights: A great introduction to the lower Latah Creek/Highbridge Park area. Also, a new pedestrian/bike bridge is planned to span the Spokane River near the start of this ride; it's significant because it will connect Fish Lake Trail (the gravel rail bed part of this ride) to Centennial Trail, allowing continuous biking from Coeur d'Alene to Cheney, and beyond.

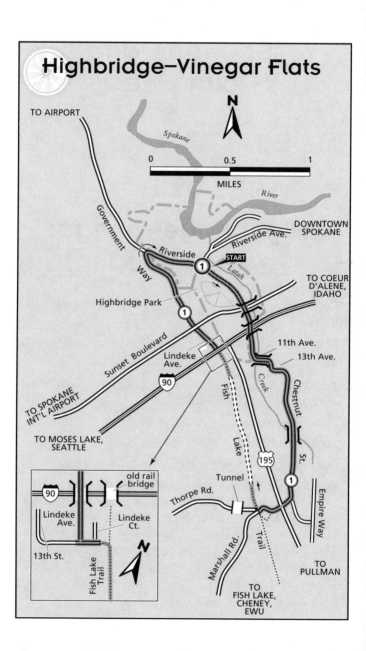

Highbridge–Vinegar Flats

TO AIRPORT

Spokane

River

N

0   0.5   1

MILES

DOWNTOWN SPOKANE

Government Way

Riverside

Riverside Ave.

START 1

Latah

TO COEUR D'ALENE, IDAHO

Highbridge Park

1

Sunset Boulevard

11th Ave.

13th Ave.

Lindeke Ave.

90

Fish

Creek

Chestnut St.

TO SPOKANE INT'L AIRPORT

TO MOSES LAKE, SEATTLE

Lake

195

1

Empire Way

Tunnel

Thorpe Rd.

Marshall Rd.

Trail

TO PULLMAN

TO FISH LAKE, CHENEY, EWU

old rail bridge

90

Lindeke Ave.

Lindeke Ct.

13th St.

Fish Lake Trail

N

Land status: City streets and trail.

Maps: USGS Spokane SW.

Access: From downtown Spokane, go west on Riverside Avenue. Within a mile, this descends a hill and leads to the main entrance of Highbridge Park, just after the bridge that spans Latah Creek. Turn in and park at Highbridge Park; the ride starts from the front entrance.

The Ride

0.0 Start from the intersection of A Street and Riverside Avenue. Elevation 1,750 feet. This is the front entrance to Highbridge Park; there's also a bridge crossing Latah Creek here. Pedal east on oiled gravel park road that is closest to Latah Creek. Grade rises gently.

0.3 Pass picnic area, a shady lawn on right. Bumps and ruts here.

0.5 Pass under the high bridges (hence, the name of the park); the first is Sunset Boulevard; the second is Interstate 90; the third is a train bridge.

0.7+ Go left at the 11th Avenue bridge; it's a low, railed concrete structure that crosses Latah Creek.

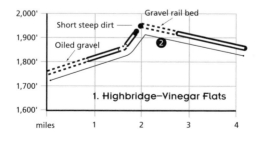

1. Highbridge–Vinegar Flats

0.8+ Turn right on Coeur d'Alene (paved now). Go two blocks and turn left at 13th Avenue. You're in Vinegar Flats now, a Spokane neighborhood with a scent of the 1960s.

1.0+ Turn right on Chestnut; glide to bridge crossing Latah Creek. Don't miss Kop Construction's park-like setting, complete with totem pole, just before the bridge.

1.3 Cross Latah Creek and bridge, and begin gentle climb.

1.6 Chestnut's pavement deteriorates briefly to gravel here; grade becomes moderate. Elevation 1,820 feet.

1.7+ Go right and uphill onto Thorpe Road; moderate grade.

1.9 Cross Washington Highway 195. Caution! This divided four-laner has traffic approaching at 70 mph! Pedal another 100 yards to rail line. At raised railroad bed (Thorpe continues through tunnel ahead), go left up singletrack game trail/footpath. It's soft and sandy, and it's best to push or carry your bike here.

2.0 On top of railroad bed go right (Fish Lake is to left). Loose gravel is the predominant surface while you're on the bed. It's a flat grade but tricky. Elevation 1,990 feet.

2.7 Cross over low rail steel and concrete bridge. Caution here!

2.8 Railroad bed deteriorates here with two kelly humps for good measure.
Note: Plans for the near future call for this section to be paved, so these obstacles and loose gravel may be gone.

2.9 Lindeke Avenue and Lindeke Court meet here (on left) creating a little-known access point to this trail. Proceed left onto pavement, and then right onto Lindeke Avenue.

3.1 Bridge now crosses I–90 as Lindeke turns to Government Way. Crest and glide to intersection of Sunset Boulevard and Government Way.

3.2 Cross Sunset and proceed on wide paved path following Government Way. You've actually regained the old rail bed you were on previously, but it's paved over here.

3.5 Begin downhill with concrete parapet on right.

3.8+ Make a sharp right at Riverside Avenue, cruising downhill.

4.2 Complete loop at Highbridge Park on right.

Rimrock– Palisades Loop

Location: West of downtown Spokane about 3 miles.

Distance: 7-mile loop.

Time: 30–45 minutes.

Tread: 1.9 miles pavement, 5.1 miles dirt/gravel road.

Aerobic level: Easy.

Technical difficulty: 1–2.

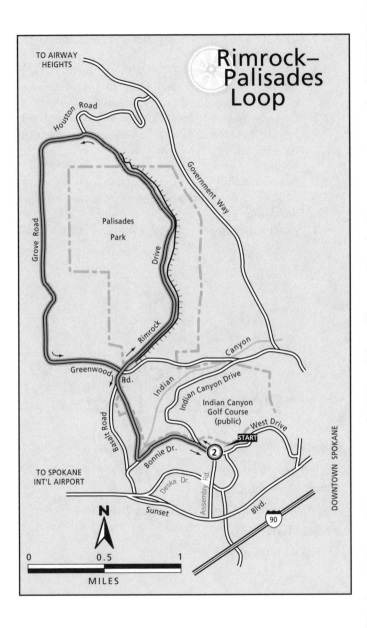

TO AIRWAY
HEIGHTS

Houston Road

Grove Road

Government Way

Palisades
Park

Rimrock Drive

Canyon

Greenwood Rd.

Indian

Indian Canyon Drive

Basalt Road

Indian Canyon
Golf Course
(public)

West Drive

START

Bonnie Dr.

2

TO SPOKANE
INT'L AIRPORT

Deska Dr.

Assembly Rd.

Sunset

Blvd.

90

DOWNTOWN SPOKANE

Rimrock–
Palisades
Loop

N

0   0.5   1

MILES

Hazards: Traffic at some intersections, some rough spots in dirt roads.

Highlights: Great views of town, easy access from west end.

Land status: County roads.

Maps: USGS Spokane SW, Airway Heights; Spokane County road map.

Access: From Sunset Boulevard west of downtown, turn right on Government Way, then left on Indian Canyon Drive. Follow this up curves to Indian Canyon Golf Course front gate, on left. Start from the gate.

The Ride

0.0   From front gate at Indian Canyon Golf Course (public), go right (down) on Indian Canyon Drive (paved). Caution! This road gets swift traffic. Round a curve.

0.1+ Turn left at Bonnie Drive (gravel), which is mostly level, rolling with scattered pines.

0.7- Turn right at Rimrock Drive (gravel), which hugs the plateau rim; trees open up.

1.3   Cross Greenwood Road (paved), jog left then right, staying on Rimrock. Caution here: traffic! Rimrock Conservation Land on left. Slight rise and curve.

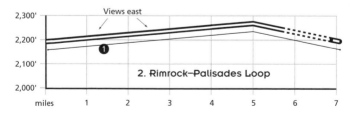

2. Rimrock–Palisades Loop

2.3 Climb small hill (great views of downtown to east).

2.7+ Cross under power lines and past sign that indicates Palisades Park (county) to left.

3.4- Go left at Houston Road. This rises through a short S curve (gravel).

3.8 Small rise and then glide.

4.0 Houston Road turns to Grove Road (paved); follow straight ahead. Mission Road goes right here.

5.2 Turn left at Greenwood Road (paved). Old school-house here on right.

5.3 Climb small rise.

5.5 Glide and cruise.

5.7 Turn right onto Rimrock (gravel): This is the way you came.

6.4 Go left at Bonnie Drive.

6.9 Go right at Indian Canyon Drive (paved). Caution, again: traffic!

7.0 Complete loop at golf course parking lot entrance gate.

Pine Bluff Loop

Location: Riverside State Park northwest of Spokane, just west of Nine Mile Dam.

Distance: 7.2 miles.

Time: 30–60 minutes.

Tread: 1.7 miles singletrack, 2 miles doubletrack, 3.0 miles county gravel, 0.5 miles pavement.

Aerobic level: Moderate.

Technical difficulty: 3, plus a couple of 4+ sections.

Hazards: Rocky (fixed and loose) sections, soft sand, and gravel, and in some spots a mixture of any two.

Highlights: A short but varied ride; almost completely in the trees; barring snow, ridable year-round.

Land status: State park and county road.

Maps: USGS Dartford, Washington; road map of Spokane County.

Access: From Nine Mile Falls (north of Spokane), cross Spokane River and go west on Charles Road, then make a left on Carlson Road. The ride starts from the Carlson Road trailhead at the top of a short hill. There's parking for a dozen cars. This ride begins and ends here.

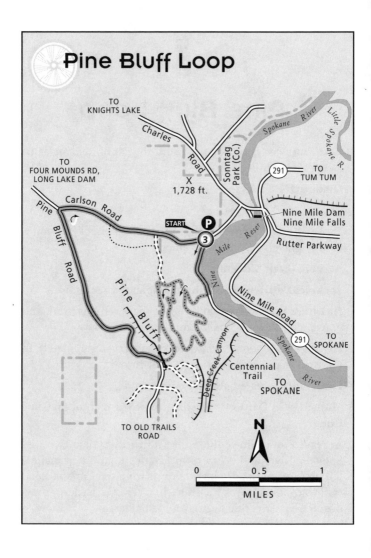

Pine Bluff Loop

TO
KNIGHTS LAKE

Charles Road

Spokane River

Little Spokane R.

TO
FOUR MOUNDS RD,
LONG LAKE DAM

Carlson Road

Sonntag Park (Co.)

X
1,728 ft.

291

TO
TUM TUM

Pine Bluff Road

START

P
3

Nine Mile Dam
Nine Mile Falls

Rutter Parkway

Pine Bluff

Nine Mile Reser

Nine Mile Road

291

TO
SPOKANE

Deep Creek Canyon

Centennial Trail

TO
SPOKANE

Spokane River

TO OLD TRAILS
ROAD

N

0   0.5   1

MILES

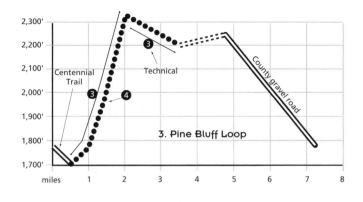

The Ride

0.0 Start from the Carlson Road Trailhead off the Centennial Trail about 9 miles north-northwest of downtown Spokane. Pedal down (east) Carlson Road (gravel) about 100 feet, then go right (south) through gate/stile to enter Centennial Trail, a paved path. Elevation 1,770 feet.

0.2 Descend short hill for a quick cruise. Potties on right.

0.3 Bottom out and begin climb just above Spokane River.

0.5 Go right at singletrack dirt that heads up an increasing grade.

0.6 Singletrack goes steep, rocky.

0.8 Wind around a 50-foot-high basalt column.

0.9 At a saddle, go left and up steep. Elevation 1,750 feet.

1.0 Climb to a grassy crest.

1.1 Negotiate some tricky basalt.

1.2 Dive into a basalt gully that then goes very rocky and technical as you climb out—4+ difficulty.

27

1.3 Climb steeply to the right; grade and difficulty then mellow as you gain some pines again.

1.4 Go left (southwest) at fork; singletrack is a narrow, tricky 4+ here, rocky again. Elevation 1,980 feet.

1.7 Cut sidehill across a couple of talus fields, climbing moderately.

1.8 Great basalt rocks here! Smell the terrain.

1.9 Trail winds around to ridgetop now. View southeast to Spokane is superb. Elevation 2,230 feet.

2.0 Climb gentle grade northwest to summit, 2,350 feet.

2.1 Bear right toward rim (park bench is visible just ahead) and follow rocky singletrack as it leaves the ridgetop.

2.2 Pass under power lines and active osprey nest. Trail turns to doubletrack briefly now.

2.3 Descend a wild, winding singletrack trail!

2.4 Trail gets rocky, 3 difficulty.

2.5 Surface mellows, then negotiate a switchback.

2.7- Loop back to fork from mile 1.4; go left, down steep hill, and then through a tight switchback left (4+).

2.8 Come to a gully bottom.

2.9 Trail goes rocky.

3.1 Go left at fork (you came in from the right).

3.2 Go left and up; grade climbs moderately and steadily.

3.4 Go left at larger road switchback and up another moderate grade.

3.7 Grade levels at 2,210 feet; you're heading south now.

4.2 Trail now turns back north; then go through gate at Pine Bluff Road. Follow gravel road to right. Elevation 2,250 feet.

4.8 Cruise and climb gently to 2,280 feet.

5.9 Go right on Carlson Road down some steep ball-bearing-style gravel. Caution!

7.0 Negotiate sweeping curve. Note the park gate to the right; stay left to the main trail.

7.2 Complete loop at starting point.

Deep Creek Loop

Location: Riverside State Park northwest of Spokane, just north of Seven Mile Bridge.

Distance: 5.2-mile loop.

Time: 25–40 minutes.

Tread: 0.3 mile singletrack, 2.4 miles doubletrack, 2.5 miles pavement.

Aerobic level: Easy to moderate.

Technical difficulty: 3-, with a small 4+ section.

Hazards: The few technical parts are difficult mostly due to the soft sand and the crossing of Deep Creek itself; if it's spring, consider a fast water (not dry) crossing.

Highlights: This is a short but mixed ride through a mini-canyon; check out the overlook at mile 1.4. There are connections from this loop that lead both north and south, if you take the time to learn the tricks of this remarkable cleft in the earth.

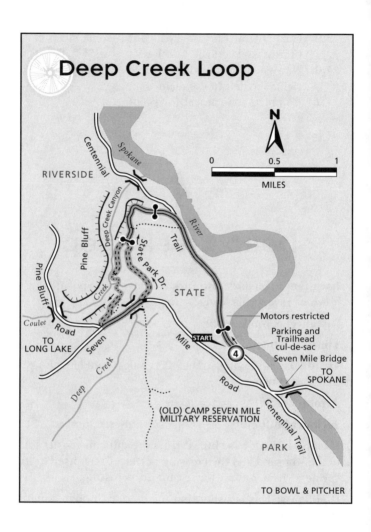

Deep Creek Loop

RIVERSIDE

Centennial

Spokane

N

0   0.5   1

MILES

Deep Creek Canyon

Pine Bluff

State Park Dr.

Trail

Creek

STATE

Pine Bluff

Coulee

Road

Seven

Creek

Motors restricted

Parking and
Trailhead
cul-de-sac

Seven Mile Bridge

TO
LONG LAKE

Deep Creek

Mile

START

④

Road

TO
SPOKANE

Centennial Trail

(OLD) CAMP SEVEN MILE
MILITARY RESERVATION

PARK

TO BOWL & PITCHER

Land status: Riverside State Park land.

Maps: Road map of Spokane County (county engineer); USGS Airway Heights, Nine Mile Falls, Washington.

Access: From the Seven Mile Bridge on the west side of the Spokane River, go north about a half mile on Riverside State Park Drive to the trailhead. There's parking for a dozen cars. This ride begins and ends here at the Seven Mile State Park trailhead, on the Centennial Trail.

The Ride

0.0 Start from the Seven Mile trailhead on the Centennial Trail just north of Seven Mile Road. Head north on the paved pathway, rolling and descending slightly. Elevation 1,680 feet.

0.8 Begin climbing easy to moderate hill.

0.9 Basalt tower on right.

1.0 Go left at fork in pavement and up moderate hill. Sign indicates Deep Creek Canyon. You're leaving the Centennial Trail.

1.1 Pass through gate and bollards on paved path; this is the Deep Creek Canyon trailhead.

1.2 Grade drops slightly.

1.4 Canyon overlook is to the right. Stay left to main trail as it degrades to sand/gravel.

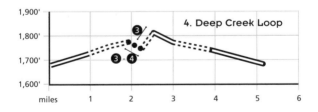

1.6 Note the singletrack that plunges down to the right here; this leads to the canyon bottom and is not really suitable for bikes. Stay left to main trail. Elevation 1,780 feet.

1.9 Pass through gate/stile as you enter the Deep Creek Overlook trailhead; autos can access this via Seven Mile Road. About 50 yards past the gate, go right off the main road down a wide, steep singletrack that leads down into the canyon (3-).

2.1 Cross Deep Creek bottom; in spring this may require a bouldery ford. Very soft sand and big rocks here. This is the technical part of this ride. Climb a steep, soft singletrack heading up through thick woods. For most, this will be a push, not a pedal (4+). Just right (north) is where Deep Creek joins Coulee Creek.

2.2 Reach a saddle and head right and up a soft, sandy rise. It's doubletrack now.

2.5 Go through rail fence and then left at Pine Bluff Road (county gravel). This is the top of this ride at 1,830 feet. Pine Bluff Road meets Seven Mile Road (paved) here; head left and down pavement. Caution! Cars come whipping by here at freeway speeds; a great glide, though.

2.8 Cross over Deep Creek bridge and begin a short climb.

3.0 Go left off pavement and onto State Park Drive (sand/dirt). Grade is level now.

3.3 Go back through gate/stile by which you came; you're back in the park.

3.9 Rejoin pavement.

4.2 Pass by overlook and plunge down hill.

4.3 Go right at Centennial Trail, cruise.

5.2 Complete loop where you started.

Wilbur Road Loop

Location: Riverside State Park, northwest of Spokane, just south of Seven Mile Bridge.

Distance: 7.3-mile loop.

Time: 40–75 minutes.

Tread: 1.2 miles singletrack, 5.9 miles forest road/gravel, 0.2 mile pavement.

Aerobic level: Moderate.

Technical difficulty: 2+ to 3.

Hazards: Rocky (fixed and loose) sections, soft sand and gravel, and in some spots a mixture of any two; large puddles or ice in freezing weather.

Highlights: A short but highly varied ride, from pavement to tricky singletrack. This loop can be ridden most of the year, if it's a mild winter; otherwise, watch for ice.

Land status: Riverside State Park land.

Maps: USGS Spokane NW.

Access: Go northwest out of Spokane on Nine Mile Road to Seven Mile Road, heading west across the Seven Mile bridge. From the Seven Mile Bridge on the west side of the Spokane River, go south about a half mile on the Aubrey White Parkway to the Wilbur Road trailhead on the Centennial Trail. There's parking for a dozen cars. This ride begins and ends here.

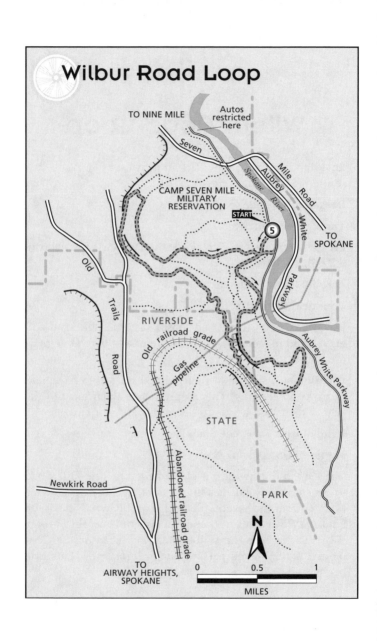

Wilbur Road Loop

TO NINE MILE

Autos restricted here

Seven

Spokane River

Aubrey White

Mile Road

CAMP SEVEN MILE MILITARY RESERVATION

START

5

TO SPOKANE

Old

Trails

Road

Parkway

RIVERSIDE

Old railroad grade

Aubrey White Parkway

Gas pipeline

STATE

Newkirk Road

Abandoned railroad grade

PARK

N

TO AIRWAY HEIGHTS, SPOKANE

0   0.5   1

MILES

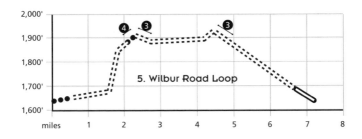

5. Wilbur Road Loop

The Ride

0.0 Start from the Wilbur Road trailhead on the Centennial Trail. If you drive in, then you're coming from the north side of the parking loop; a singletrack leads off through pines to the right (southwest). Follow this as it starts on level ground. Do not take the singletrack hard right under the power lines. Elevation 1,640 feet.

0.1 Bear left at a singletrack fork.

0.2 Go right at gravel road where the pines open up a bit. This is now the old Camp Seven Mile (Civilian Conservation Corps). Stay left now, at intersecting roads from right.

0.4 Bear left at fork in road; it gets bumpy as you hug the edge of the trees.

0.5- Stay left at fork and do not head toward meadow.

0.6 Stay right to more heavily traveled doubletrack.

0.8 Cross an east-west road, staying southeast and generally straight ahead.

1.0 Come back close to Aubrey White Parkway (paved Centennial Trail here) keeping to gravel/dirt doubletrack that then veers away right.

1.3 Pass through a recent burn area.

1.4 Stay straight to doubletrack and do not climb hill.

1.7- Stay to doubletrack dirt as it reenters trees.

1.7+ Begin winding up a steepening grade; soft gravel and ruts (3-).

1.8 Gain a gravelly ridge and vista south. Stay right and continue climbing. You're now heading toward the rimrock cliffs. Elevation 1,850 feet.

2.0+ Steep gravel road crests, then cruises toward rocks and burn area. Bear right after passing first trees; do not take straight ahead fork.

2.2 At rimrock base begin steep and rocky climb up singletrack. The basalt here is somewhat polished and angular. This is perhaps the crux of this ride (4-).

2.3 Reach small crest. Elevation 1,910 feet. Two more small dips and knobs are tricky and fun over the next quarter of a mile, all very rocky and technical (3).

2.6 Watch for a quick, rocky drop here! Follow it to easier ground.

3.0 Bear left as trail descends into saddle and straight at bottom of grade.

3.1 Bear right where wide track (now forest road) splits. (Left will take you onto Marchand Road which leads to ORV [off road vehicle] parking lot on Old Trails Road.) This winds around right.

3.2+ Cross gravel trail and proceed toward top of gully.

3.3- Do not proceed into gully; rather, bear left at gully.

3.5 Cross gravel/dirt road.

4.2 Rise up to Old Trails Road (two-lane, gravel) and pass through park Gate 24 and stile. Proceed right (north) on Old Trails Road.

4.3 Go right through Gate 26 off Old Trails and down a moderately steep and very rocky/gravelly doubletrack (3-). Did I mention the ruts? Views at the top, too.

4.8 Go right at hill bottom and follow level forest road south.

5.0	Go right when you meet a dirt forest road. Watch for puddles or ice in here.
5.8	Go left at fork, keeping to doubletrack.
6.3	Continue left at split, which then leads to a clearing.
6.5	Stay on doubletrack, bearing left.
6.6	Make a sharp right, staying on dirt doubletrack.
7.0	Come to a junction of several roads. An old military bunker is ahead. Go left.
7.1	Go left at pavement (Aubrey White Parkway section of the Centennial Trail). Cruise back to complete loop at 7.3 miles.

Wilbur–Bowl and Pitcher Long Loop

Location: Riverside State Park, northwest of Spokane, just south of Seven Mile Bridge.

Distance: 9.8-mile loop.

Time: 50–75 minutes.

Tread: 4.4 miles singletrack, 5.4 miles forest road/doubletrack.

Aerobic level: Moderate.

Technical difficulty: 2–4.

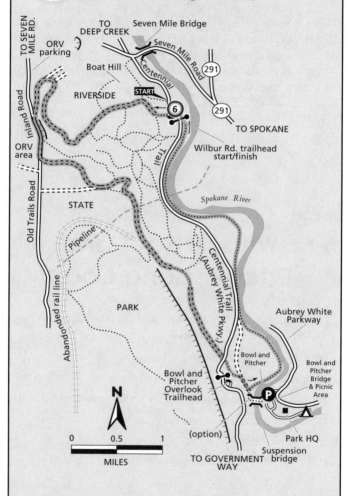

Wilbur–Bowl and Pitcher Long Loop

TO SEVEN MILE RD.

ORV parking

TO DEEP CREEK

Seven Mile Bridge

Seven Mile Road

291

Boat Hill

Centennial

RIVERSIDE

START

6

291

TO SPOKANE

Wilbur Rd. trailhead start/finish

Inland Road

ORV area

Trail

Spokane River

Old Trails Road

STATE

Pipeline

Abandonded rail line

PARK

Centennial Trail (Aubrey White Pkwy.)

Aubrey White Parkway

Bowl and Pitcher

Bowl and Pitcher Bridge & Picnic Area

P

N

Bowl and Pitcher Overlook Trailhead

0   0.5   1

MILES

(option)

Park HQ

Suspension bridge

TO GOVERNMENT WAY

Hazards: Rocky (fixed and loose) sections, soft sand and gravel, and in some spots a mixture of any two. Mile 5.8 is a very hazardous crossing of the Centennial Trail.

Highlights: A highly varied ride: cruising to gnarly. This ride starts with cruising and climbing, and ends with fun singletrack!

Land status: Riverside State Park.

Maps: USGS Spokane SW.

Access: From the Seven Mile Bridge on the west side of the Spokane River, go south about a half mile on the Aubrey White Parkway to the Wilbur Road trailhead. There's parking for a dozen cars. This ride begins and ends here.

The Ride

0.0 From the Wilbur Road trailhead on the Centennial Trail, head west on a singletrack that takes off into the pines between two other singletracks. The trail is smooth and flat.

0.1 Go right onto a dirt forest road; you're heading north now straight and flat as you enter a big meadow. Elevation 1,780 feet.

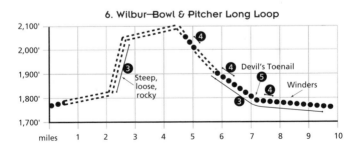

6. Wilbur–Bowl & Pitcher Long Loop

0.4+ Make a sharp left onto another dirt doubletrack. Enter trees at the base of a hill.

0.5+ Take a doubletrack right and up a steep grade that's mostly loose, round rock.

0.6 At top of grade go right on gravel road in meadow. Elevation 1,860 feet.

0.7+ At fork, stay right on the track that hugs the rim.

1.2 At a couple of loops that split left, stay to the right.

2.1 Go left onto a smaller doubletrack. Elevation 1,840 feet.

2.2 Go left at base of hill and start to climb moderately.

2.5 Grade turns soft and steep and goes to 3.

2.7- Top out at state park Gate 26, Inland Road. Go left on Inland Road (gravel). The main ORV staging area is just visible about a quarter of a mile to the right (west). Elevation 2,100 feet.

2.8 Go left, off of Inland Road, through Gate 24, and onto a forest doubletrack. This is great cruising through curves and on a changeable surface (2+).

3.4 Stay straight ahead on main track as a doubletrack intersects this one.

3.7+ At a pronounced, narrow gully, either go sharp left (out) and through the gully, or swing around wider through the hairpin, and stay to the main line you've been on.

3.9 Sweep around a curve and climb a short, rocky hill.

4.0 Climb a short, steep hill, and then stay right to main trail a bit farther.

4.4 Climb up steeply as it winds around to the right on basalt.

4.5 Top out, grade levels, then glide a bit. You're at 1,990 feet.

4.6+ Climb to summit of ride at 2,020 feet. Then swoop quickly as track hugs rimrock base 40 feet to your right.

4.7 Glide briefly and then descend a steep, rocky chute. Caution (4+)!

4.9 Go right onto singletrack.

5.2- Merge with rolling forest road.

5.7- Go through sweeping S turns, then descend.

5.8+ Merge with another doubletrack right, hugging the rimrock base. At state park Gate 38, cross paved Centennial Trail. Caution! Be sure to check out the traffic, especially from the right (south); wheels of all kinds zoom down this rocket ramp, sometimes exceeding 30 mph, and sometimes accompanied by people. Pick up singletrack directly across as it dives into forest (2+).

6.1 This is a rocky, technical cruiser. S turn is tight (4-).

6.2 Dive down to Bowl and Pitcher notch. As you cross a dirt forest road, bear left to stay to singletrack, heading toward Spokane River. Option: Two-tenths of a mile to the right on this dirt forest road is the Bowl and Pitcher Bridge and Picnic Area.

6.8 Stay right to main rocky trail hugging riverbank downstream.

7.1+ Devil's Toenail (the name for rapids/rocks on the Spokane River) is visible to the right. Negotiate a winding, rocky section before a brief climb (3).

7.2+ Go right at a three-way fork, keeping to singletrack. This is the Devil's Toenail. Begin area of sharp, broken rock.

7.3+ Large, sharp, and loose rock in a narrow confine. It's courteous and safe to walk, as there is usually an abundance of foot traffic (5). Then cruise tight curves close to basalt faces; some exposure and limited visibility (3). Elevation 1,860 feet.

7.5 Trail turns rocky and smooth.

7.6+ Climb loose gravel up a moderate (4) hill. Stay to singletrack as it rises next to and falls away from the

Centennial Trail. Then cruise on a smooth ribbon laced with ankle-biting boulders (3-)!

8.5 Go right at singletrack Y, then, in a subtle saddle, negotiate rocky S turns (3+).

8.6 Enter a soft, sandy, grassy area.

9.2 Cruise through some technical curves (3).

9.4 Climb a rocky, short hill.

9.7 Keep left to main track as it climbs up to Centennial Trail.

9.8 Complete loop at Wilbur Road trailhead.

Seven Mile Loop

Location: Riverside State Park, 7 miles northwest of downtown Spokane.

Distance: 7.3-mile loop.

Time: 40–50 minutes.

Tread: 4.7 miles forest road/doubletrack, 2.6 miles pavement.

Aerobic level: Moderate.

Technical difficulty: 2+ off pavement.

Hazards: Traffic on Seven Mile Road and Inland Road, foot and wheel traffic on Centennial Trail.

Highlights: This is mostly an easy cruiser with some fun, smooth sections of singletrack.

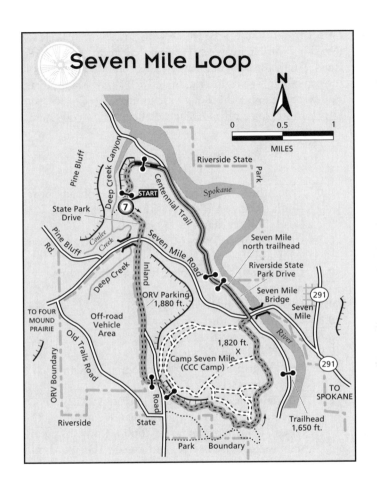

Seven Mile Loop

0   0.5   1

MILES

Pine Bluff

Deep Creek Canyon

Riverside State Park

Spokane

START

Centennial Trail

State Park Drive

Pine Bluff Rd.

Coulee Creek

Seven Mile Road

Seven Mile north trailhead

Riverside State Park Drive

Seven Mile Bridge

Seven Mile

291

Deep Creek

Inland

ORV Parking 1,880 ft.

River

TO FOUR MOUND PRAIRIE

Off-road Vehicle Area

Old Trails Road

1,820 ft. X

Camp Seven Mile (CCC Camp)

291

TO SPOKANE

ORV BOUNDARY

Road

Trailhead 1,650 ft.

Riverside   State

Park   Boundary

Land status: Riverside State Park land.

Maps: USGS Airway Heights; Road map of Spokane County; good city map.

Access: From downtown Spokane, take Monroe Street north to Northwest Boulevard, then right on Cochran, left onto Driscoll Boulevard, which runs into Nine Mile Road (Washington Highway 291), and left onto Seven Mile Road. Cross the Spokane River and go about 1.5 miles; at the top of a hill go right onto State Park Drive (sandy, dirt). Follow this about a third of a mile to the Deep Creek Overlook parking lot/trailhead. The ride begins and ends here.

The Ride

0.0 From the Deep Creek Overlook trailhead, pedal south on State Park Drive (dirt) toward Seven Mile Road. Mileage starts from Gate 29.

0.3+ Go right onto Seven Mile Road (paved). Caution! Watch for fast-moving traffic.

0.4 Go left onto Inland Road. It's sand/dirt and rises up briefly.

0.5 Crest as surface turns to gravel.

0.6 Cross under four sets of power lines.

0.8 Enter ORV (off-road vehicle) area (sign on right).

0.9 Climb short, moderate hill.

1.1 Pass by main ORV parking/staging area (on left); potties here.

1.2 Go right, passing through the main ORV fence opening, then go left immediately and hug the fence, continuing south. You're now following Inland Road as before, but inside the wood rail fence. Watch for dirt bikes and ATVs in here.

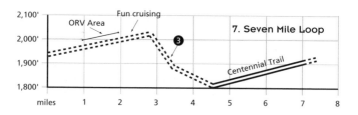

1.9 Go left through wood rail fence and leave ORV area. Follow doubletrack along forest edge.

2.1+ Go through gate and then cross Inland/Old Trails Road.

2.2 Pass around Gate 24 and onto a forest road. Regain forest. The next one-third mile is some great cruising fun.

2.8- Pass a sign for the military reservation on left (old Camp Seven Mile); then at a three-way split, take the middle fork, which is mostly level and grassy. Elevation 2,020 feet.

2.9+ Go through a rocky compression dip.

3.0 Grade bottoms out, curves.

3.1- Make a sharp left down a gully bottom. At this juncture, at least two other tracks head straight, right, and up.

3.2- Surface gets rocky and rutted (3); grade drops moderately.

3.3 Bear left onto a gravel forest road, splitting from the present track. Elevation 1,900 feet.

3.4 Merge with wider road in the flats.

3.6 Bear right at open meadow. This is a Civilian Conservation Corps camp where three roads cross. Follow the right, most obvious track directly into the pines. Then go left on a smooth, dirt forest road on a slight rise.

3.8+ Go left at Y.

3.9 Bear left again at split, cruising.

4.2+ Take slight left on rolling forest road. (Sharp left climbs up a gravelly track, and right goes off into a clearing.) You're hugging a bottom track, following a steep embankment on the left.

4.4 Go right as you come to a juncture where a private drive goes left and up. To the right is a state park road (rocky and potholed) leading off through a meadow.

4.5 Go left at Centennial Trail (paved and flat).

4.6+ Go left and up (west) on Seven Mile Road. The Spokane River and the Seven Mile Bridge are just right. Elevation 1,810 feet.

4.7 Go right on Riverside State Park Drive/Centennial Trail. Cruise through stables and homes, but be aware: There are kids here, and autos share this section of roadway with bikes and nonmotorized vehicles.

5.1 Climb steep hill.

5.5 At Seven Mile north trailhead, go through stiles that bar motorized travel beyond this point. Cruise. Elevation 1,840 feet.

6.3 Climb moderate grade.

6.4+ Basalt pillar on right. Go left off Centennial Trail and up old park road, also paved.

6.6 Pass through stiles/gate as grade mellows. Elevation 1,890 feet.

6.8 Deep Creek Canyon Overlook is to the right here.

7.1 Pedestrian trail drops quickly into canyon at right here. Stay to main road straight ahead. Thinning pavement turns to dirt and gravel here.

7.3 Complete loop at Gate 29 and Deep Creek Overlook trailhead.

Bowl and Pitcher Loop

Location: Bowl and Pitcher area (parking lot/picnic site/trailhead), Riverside State Park, west of downtown Spokane.

Distance: 6.8 miles.

Time: 35–50 minutes.

Tread: 3.8 miles singletrack, 0.9 miles forest road/double-track, 2.1 miles paved, dedicated trail.

Aerobic level: Easy.

Technical difficulty: 3.

Hazards: Rocky (sharp, fixed, and loose), especially at the Devil's Toenail; one soft sand section. It's polite and diplomatic to walk the Toenail section, even if you're a trials rider who could do it on one wheel. Perhaps the most aesthetically pure piece of singletrack in the entire area, it draws heavy traffic at peak hours and should be avoided then.

Highlights: Pure singletrack; clean but not simple, this loop or parts of it can be combined, woven into other regimens. Social and well used, don't expect privacy unless you go when most don't.

Land status: Riverside State Park.

Maps: USGS Airway Heights, Spokane NW; any good Spokane city map.

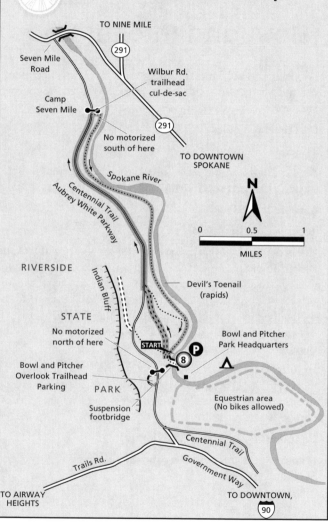

Bowl and Pitcher Loop

TO NINE MILE

(291)

Seven Mile Road

Wilbur Rd. trailhead cul-de-sac

Camp Seven Mile

(291)

No motorized south of here

TO DOWNTOWN SPOKANE

Spokane River

Centennial Trail

Aubrey White Parkway

N

0   0.5   1

MILES

RIVERSIDE

Indian Bluff

Devil's Toenail (rapids)

STATE

No motorized north of here

START

P

8

Bowl and Pitcher Park Headquarters

Bowl and Pitcher Overlook Trailhead Parking

PARK

Suspension footbridge

Equestrian area (No bikes allowed)

Centennial Trail

Trails Rd.

Government Way

TO AIRWAY HEIGHTS

TO DOWNTOWN,

(90)

Access: Bowl and Pitcher Park can be accessed from Downriver Drive or the Aubrey White Parkway (on the east or north side of the river). These two park roads merge at the park's entry. You can get to them via Northwest Boulevard and Monroe Street from downtown, or from Fort Wright Drive and Government Way from the west. There's usually ample parking in the shade. The ride begins and ends here.

The Ride

0.0   At Bowl and Pitcher Park parking lot/picnic site, cross over the Spokane River via the pedestrian suspension bridge.

0.1+ As the main pedestrian trail heads up right to concrete steps, stay straight ahead and up a steep, loose, and rocky gully (4). Then go right and up moderate rise as you meet a larger, contouring trail. (To the left is closed to bikes.) This curves you around and behind a wood/shake picnic shelter.

0.2   Pass an outhouse and go through a gap in basalt towers to either side. This is forest road now.

0.3   Under dense canopy, stay straight ahead to main forest road. A singletrack intersects the forest road here.

0.9   Climb gentle to moderate grade.

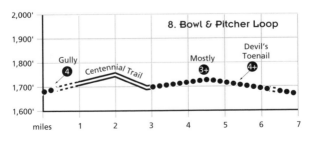

1.0 Go right on Centennial Trail (paved). Cruise the next 2 miles of smooth, dedicated trail. Beware of heavy traffic at times!

1.7 Climb moderate hill.

2.0 Crest and glide.

3.1 Come to Wilbur Road trailhead. Pass through stiles and then head immediately right onto a dirt single-track. Your warm-up's over; get ready to exercise that front shock! Follow this as it drops 20 feet onto mostly level and quickly changing trail (2).

3.3 Enter tight curves, bigger rocks (2+).

3.4 Fixed boulders (3).

3.6 Track widens, cruise.

3.9 Go through a grassy opening and then negotiate some tricky (3) boulders as the track narrows.

4.0 Soft sand.

4.1 Climb short.

4.2 Climb rocky technical section (3).

4.3 Continue up, soft, then stay left to main track.

4.8 Rifle Club is across river now.

5.0 Enter burn area.

5.1+ Rise up gravelly track to Centennial Trail; stay on singletrack as it drops back down a section of loose, round rocks (3).

5.4 Trail narrows as you wind around some basalt faces. Track becomes somewhat exposed as it leads you close to and above the water. Go from 2+ to 5 as you enter the Devil's Toenail (the name for a rapid and rock formation on the Spokane River). The trail has been tamed somewhat by the hands of humans, but it has retained its character as a rock garden: sharp, loose, and slick when wet. It's best to WALK (yes, I know it's a four-letter word) this section.

5.5 Rise up to a basalt column overlook (4). The Toenail is presented to you here in full symphonic stereo-vision.

5.6 Bear down and left at three-way fork, continuing upstream. Terrain opens; midring cruising ahead.

6.5 After bearing right on main track, go left at forest road in full canopy of trees. Road also goes right, and singletrack climbs steeply ahead. This is the northern entry to the Bowl and Pitcher area. Basalt columns rise up to either side as you pass through and out of the thicker trees.

6.6+ Pass outhouse, walk or ride carefully down two sets of steps, also passing a wood/shake picnic shelter. Lots of hikers, tourists, and gawkers here during summers and weekends, so be aware! The access you save may be your own.

6.7 Cross Bowl and Pitcher Bridge (a replica of a 1930s Civilian Conservation Corps pedestrian suspension bridge).

6.8 On east side of river and bridge now, enter the Bowl and Pitcher parking lot and trailhead, and complete loop.

Bowl and Pitcher: Boat Hill

Location: Bowl and Pitcher area (parking lot/picnic site/trailhead), Riverside State Park, west of downtown Spokane.

Distance: 5.4 miles plus two loop options that would make the total either 8.1 or 9.1 miles.

Time: 20–35 minutes.

Tread: 2 miles singletrack, 3.4 miles forest road/double-track. Loop options paved or singletrack.

Aerobic level: Easy.

Technical difficulty: 3.

Hazards: Rocky (sharp, fixed, and loose) especially at the Devil's Toenail; one soft sand section. It's polite and diplomatic to walk the Toenail section, even if you're a trials rider who could do it on one wheel. Perhaps the most aesthetically pure piece of singletrack in the entire area, it draws heavy traffic at peak hours and should be avoided then.

Highlights: This route starts with pure singletrack—mixed and varied, and finishes with superlative forest road cruising, but not without an occasional technical obstacle to challenge you. The combined effect is sustained fun!

Land status: Riverside State Park.

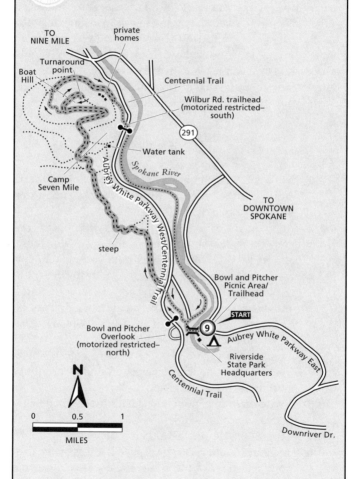

Bowl and Pitcher: Boat Hill

TO
NINE MILE

private homes

Turnaround point

Boat Hill

Centennial Trail

Wilbur Rd. trailhead
(motorized restricted–
south)

291

Water tank

Spokane River

Camp
Seven Mile

Aubrey White Parkway West/Centennial Trail

TO
DOWNTOWN
SPOKANE

steep

Bowl and Pitcher
Picnic Area/
Trailhead

START

9

Bowl and Pitcher
Overlook
(motorized restricted–
north)

Aubrey White Parkway East

Riverside
State Park
Headquarters

Centennial Trail

N

0   0.5   1

MILES

Downriver Dr.

Maps: USGS Airway Heights, Spokane NW; any good Spokane city map.

Access: Bowl and Pitcher area can be accessed from Downriver Drive or the Aubrey White Parkway (on the east or north side of the river). These two park roads merge at the park's entry. You can get to them via Northwest Boulevard and Monroe Street from downtown or from Fort Wright Drive and Government Way from the west. There's usually ample parking in the shade. The ride begins and ends here, at the parking lot by the suspension bridge.

The Ride

0.0 At Bowl and Pitcher Park parking lot/trailhead, cross over the Spokane River via the pedestrian suspension bridge. Elevation 1,660 feet.

0.1+ As the main pedestrian trail heads up right to concrete steps, stay straight ahead and up a steep, loose, and rocky gully (4). Then go right and up a moderate rise as you meet a larger, contouring trail. (To the left is closed to bikes.) This curves you around and behind a wood/shake picnic shelter. Pass an outhouse and go through a gap in basalt towers to either side. This is forest road now.

0.2+ Under a dense canopy, go left and up a steep singletrack. This rocky trail snakes around as it climbs away from the forest road.

0.3 Grade eases to a moderate sidehill trail. Then negotiate a sweeping winder (3+).

0.4 Crest at basalt overlook, then cruise.

0.6 Come to Centennial Trail (paved). Cross with caution! Speeders of all kinds streak down from the left. (Have you ever seen a 40 mph roller-stroller?

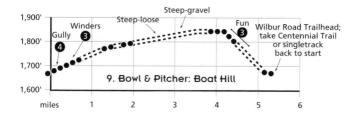

9. Bowl & Pitcher: Boat Hill

The point is, you may not.) Crossing the paved pathway, proceed onto forest road at Gatepost 38. Smooth and level now.

0.7 Go left at Y up steep grade, a wide doubletrack now.

0.8- Tricky curves (3) as you enter a burn area.

1.3 Go left onto singletrack as track turns level through meadows. Elevation 1,740 feet.

1.5+ Merge left with forest road, climbing gently.

1.6 Climb steep, rocky chute. This is solid 4. Watch out for downhill traffic!

1.7+ Crest at 1,790 feet, at just under 1.7, and dive as track turns into a wide cruiser. Take a sharp right into a well-defined gully, which then drops moderately into a rocky, rutted 3- road.

1.9 Stay to main road, then dip and climb up a small incline, which then leads to an open meadow and a three-way fork. Take middle fork.

2.0 Go left at doubletrack split.

2.2 Go left away from trees at another split.

2.4 Wind around to base of hill, bearing right and north.

2.5 Take a sharp left up gravelly doubletrack. This is steep, loose, and 3.

2.6 Crest top of hill. Go right at three-way split. Cruise and glide.

3.0 Go right at Y, turning to wide, open road.

3.1 Go left up steep, soft gravel hill.

3.4 Crest hill (1,840 feet) and stay right to main doubletrack. But also note on the way back you'll be riding on a barely visible singletrack just straight ahead to the left of the larger track you're following now. This is the top of Boat Hill.

3.6 This is the turnaround point. There are views of the river and Seven Mile Bridge. You'll backtrack the last two-tenths of a mile.

3.8 Go right onto a thin singletrack just west of where you crested this hill. Grassy hummocks give way to small pines and a narrow, rocky, descending trail (3).

4.0 A sharp right leads into a meadow. Caution: If this is wet, please jump off your bike and leave no track. Elevation 1,830 feet. Grade eases now to gentle descent and fun, technical gliding (3-).

4.3 Grade drops again!

4.4 Go right onto smooth forest road. Pines are small and thick in here.

4.6 Pass three houses (private homes) to your right. Share road this section.

4.8 Go left into meadow on park access road. Then after 50 feet, go right onto a smooth, straight dirt road, which almost looks like an old airstrip.

5.3 Go left onto singletrack as road enters pines and starts to curve right.

5.4 Level singletrack winds to Wilbur Road trailhead.

Options here (to return to starting point) are:

1. Take Centennial Trail (paved) back to Bowl and Pitcher (turning left off paved pathway at Gatepost 38 and base of steep hill). Final mileage this way is 8.1 miles.

2. Take singletrack just left of the stiles on the Centennial Trail. This technical and fun section of trail follows the river to Bowl and Pitcher. It's described in Ride 8 from mile 3.1 on. Final mileage this way is 9.1 miles.

Bowl and Pitcher Upstream

Location: Bowl and Pitcher area (headquarters for Riverside State Park), about 5 miles northwest of downtown Spokane.

Distance: 8.8 miles, out and back.

Time: 45–90 minutes.

Tread: 5.6 miles pavement, 0.7 miles forest road/doubletrack, 2.5 miles singletrack.

Aerobic level: Easy.

Technical difficulty: 2–3, with a few 4 sections.

Hazards: Traffic on pavement; sections of narrow, rocky, and soft trail.

Highlights: This ride follows one of the most scenic sections of the Spokane River. The Bowl and Pitcher area is a magical center of the Spokane River and its system of canyons, posing sheer basalt columns against fierce white

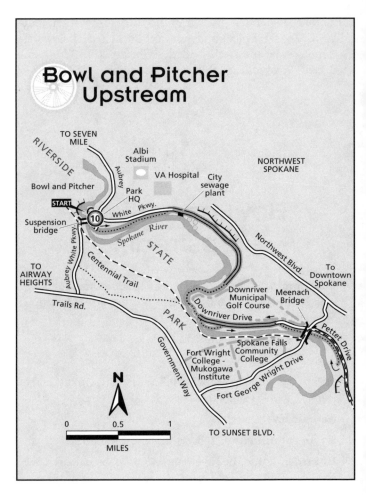

Bowl and Pitcher Upstream

TO SEVEN MILE

RIVERSIDE

Aubrey

Albi Stadium

VA Hospital

NORTHWEST SPOKANE

Bowl and Pitcher

Park HQ

City sewage plant

START

White Pkwy.

Suspension bridge

10

Spokane River

STATE

Aubrey White Pkwy.

Centennial Trail

Northwest Blvd.

TO AIRWAY HEIGHTS

To Downtown Spokane

Trails Rd.

PARK

Downriver Municipal Golf Course

Meenach Bridge

Downriver Drive

Pettet Drive

Government Way

Fort Wright College - Mukogawa Institute

Spokane Falls Community College

N

Fort George Wright Drive

0   0.5   1

TO SUNSET BLVD.

MILES

water. Just walking the trails or the suspension bridge is a thrill-packed adventure for little ones or the timid. The picnic area surrounding the parking lot is a gem, and the trailhead/bridge offers strategic access to upstream portions of the park.

Land status: Riverside State Park land and city streets.

Maps: Valley Map Spokane (Spokane Valley Chamber of Commerce); Riverside State Park Guide; USGS Spokane NW; any good Spokane street map.

Access: The Bowl and Pitcher is located about 5 miles northwest of downtown Spokane on the north (also east) side of the Spokane River. You get there from Downriver Drive via Pettet Drive or Fort George Wright Drive and Government Way. After you drive into the main entrance of the park off of Downriver Drive (west), turn right just after the registration and information booth. The ride begins and ends at the Bowl and Pitcher Picnic Area parking lot by the suspension bridge over the Spokane River.

The Ride

0.0 Pedal east out through the parking area the way you drove in. Rather than turning left up the hill to go past the information shack, continue straight ahead and level on toward the main campground. This is paved park roadway with mixed pines and firs. Elevation 1,700 feet.

0.2 Bear left on pavement as you pass the park ranger's office complex on right.

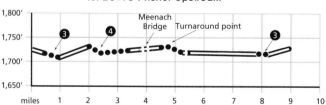

10. Bowl & Pitcher Upstream

0.3 Grade drops briefly as you enter the main campground area, which is open to camping only during the summer.

0.4 A hiking trail sign indicates a dirt singletrack trail going right, toward the river. Either take that trail or continue to the end of the paved loop and bear slightly right through Campsite 15. Follow dirt singletrack through level forest floor. (This second option may be better if the campsite is unoccupied.)

0.5 Wind through trees; narrow, fun, and rocky in spots (3).

0.6 If you went right at the trail sign, bear left now about 10 yards and pick up a wider dirt singletrack.

0.8 Rise to doubletrack.

0.9 Take left fork up steep and soft singletrack—4+ here; most will need to push their bikes.

1.0 On Downriver Drive now, go right on paved roadway. Caution! There's not a lot of shoulder here, but this is a favorite bike route. Don't rely too heavily on the good manners of drivers. Elevation 1,740 feet. Basically, you've left the security of the forest to circumvent the Spokane city sewer treatment plant, which you now skirt for the next half-mile-plus.

1.7 Hand-built Civilian Conservation Corps rock walls on left bank and great views of the river right, 150 feet below.

2.0 Enter curves and descend, cruising.

2.2 Go right down a steep, wide dirt trail and off of pavement. For the more timid, there's a thin sidehill trail just right, which will take you on a gentler slope to the bottom of this embankment. If you do plunge straight down, caution! It's soft, and I rate it at 4. Then, at bottom of bank, head left, continuing upstream on a wide, mostly level singletrack. Take the right fork then, which follows the river closely.

2.4   Merge with doubletrack from left.

2.5   Take singletrack again that splits briefly right and hugs river bank, rolling (2).

2.6   Merge with pea gravel pathway from left.

2.7+ Go right and down on singletrack. There are boulders as you follow a narrow sidehill track just above river.

2.8   Dip and rise.

2.9   Trail now turns to narrow, rocky, and flat (3) in close pines. Then climb out 30 vertical feet on sustained, difficult trail.

3.1   Climb wide gravel track, then back left onto Downriver Drive (paved) and continue right (southeast) upstream. Downriver Municipal Golf Course is to left. Cruise, with narrow shoulder.

3.7   Head right off pavement on gravel access road and through steel gate. Follow this wide, open fire lane area, staying to the rightmost track nearest the river.

3.9   The open access area ends here as the T. J. Meenach Bridge looms ahead. Head up left on a short, steep singletrack (4+). Most will need to walk this abrupt embankment, which leads to the junction of Downriver and Pettet Drives under the bridge.

4.0   Bear right (upstream) at the top of this bank and follow the dirt path that parallels the pavement to a paved parking area just east of the bridge.

4.1   Proceed through the parking area to the east (upstream) end and pass through rock barriers/stiles and onto a paved pathway descending slightly.

4.2   Pathway pavement ends, turns to dirt/gravel. There's a nice covered observation platform built out over the river's edge to the right here; it's a great place for a break or shelter, if needed. The trail for the next quarter mile narrows through thick brush and small trees, so take your time in here and be aware.

4.5+ This small open area with a fire ring and large boulders is essentially the trail's end; turn around and head back the way you came. There are at least three incipient trails that head off from here, but that will have to be a matter for your own curiosity and energy. Elevation 1,790 feet.

5.0 Heading back the way you came, go back through parking area and under bridge.

5.1 Go left down steep bank.

5.3 Head back around steel gate.

5.4 Bear left and resume Downriver Drive (paved).

6.5 Bear left at paved fork. This is the entrance of Riverside State Park and the start of the Aubrey White Parkway.

7.5 Pass Sewer City on left.

7.8 Go left down steep singletrack just past Sewer City and off pavement (3)! Then go right at bottom of embankment on singletrack (2–3).

8.1–8.2 Boulders and rocks (3) on narrow trail.

8.2+ Enter campground loop road (paved).

8.5 Go right and up small hill, then pass the park headquarters on left.

8.8 Complete ride back at Bowl and Pitcher.

Fish Lake Trail

Location: South-southwest of Spokane, between Cheney and Spokane.

Distance: 23.1 miles, out and back.

Time: 2–4 hours.

Tread: 2.2 miles paved, 20.9 miles gravel rail bed (plans are to pave the entire section of rail bed from Spokane to Fish Lake, so watch for changes in the next couple of years).

Aerobic level: Moderate.

Technical difficulty: 2–3.

Hazards: Soft gravel, small tight trees in short sections. These hazards should be eliminated in the near future as this old railroad bed receives funding and an upgraded surface. Two active rail line crossings, several private road crossings, and one county road crossing require your attention, but over the course of 11-plus miles one way, you're very protected from traffic.

Highlights: Most of this ride follows an abandoned rail line from Spokane's west end to Fish Lake. At Fish Lake, the turnaround point for this ride, you may elect to continue on the paved surface all the way to Cheney and Eastern Washington University. Who knows, maybe someday when this trail is completely paved, it will become a major bike commuter route. Two charming lakes, rolling hills and pines, along with numerous rock cliffs, tunnels, and bridges

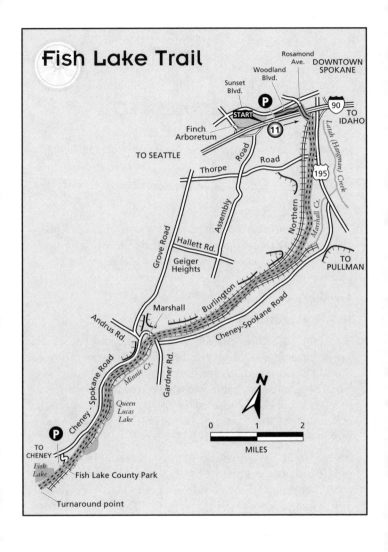

Fish Lake Trail

Sunset Blvd.

Woodland Blvd.

Rosamond Ave.

DOWNTOWN SPOKANE

P

START

Finch Arboretum

TO SEATTLE

11

90

TO IDAHO

195

Latah (Hangman) Creek

Thorpe

Road

Road

Assembly

Northern

Marshall Ct.

Grove Road

Hallett Rd.

Geiger Heights

Burlington

Marshall

Andrus Rd.

Cheney-Spokane Road

TO PULLMAN

Cheney - Spokane Road

Gardner Rd.

Minnie Cr.

Queen Lucas Lake

P

TO CHENEY

Fish Lake

Fish Lake County Park

Turnaround point

N

0   1   2

MILES

give this ride a protected and rural quality. Grades are gentle. Wildlife is abundant.

Land status: Public access trail, county roads, and city streets.

Maps: Spokane City Parks (guide and map); road map of Spokane County; USGS Spokane SW, Four Lakes, Washington; any good Spokane street map.

Access: The ride begins and ends at the Finch Arboretum (a Spokane City Park) located in southwest Spokane. To get there, proceed west on Second Avenue to Sunset Boulevard, and then turn left at Finch Arboretum, marked by a sign about a half mile uphill after crossing Government Way. Follow Woodland Boulevard around to the right where the arboretum main building and parking area are located.

The Ride

0.0 Start from Finch Arboretum main parking area, just south of main arboretum building. Head out parking lot and turn left on paved F Street. Elevation 2,080 feet.

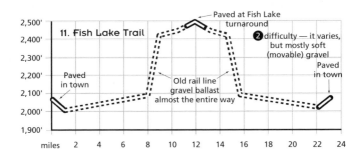

0.1   Wind around right and down as F Street turns into Woodland Boulevard.

0.4   Turn right on Rosamond Avenue and cross Interstate 90 over Rosamond bridge. Cruise down wide pavement as it winds left.

0.6   Cross under railroad bridge, then cross Lindeke Street at four-way stop. Proceeding straight ahead through this intersection (past DEAD END sign), leave pavement onto dirt; this is the north end of the Fish Lake Trail.

0.7   Go right on gravel rail bed. At present there are some earth berms (to keep motorheads out) that must be negotiated before the trail smooths out (2+).

0.9+   Cross 16th Avenue bridge (concrete and steel). Exercise caution here as the rock ballast is very loose and, at present, no guardrails exist.

1.2   Pass through basalt rock cut/escarpment. There is presently a large rockfall here that constricts the trail to a narrow, rocky slot. Elevation 2,000 feet.

1.3   Visual boundaries open up as trail proceeds on levee.

1.5   Cross Thorpe Road bridge.

1.7–1.9 Trail proceeds through basalt rock cuts.

2.1   Pass through metal gate.

2.2   Reach open meadow and farm area.

2.5   Negotiate small pines and loose ballast (2+).

2.7   Rail bed briefly is lost here (an old bridge was obviously removed). Follow singletrack through woods, bearing right along top of sandy bank. You'll pass just left of a STATE LAND sign and then plunge down a sandy trail onto county road. Cross road.

2.8   Regain rail bed by climbing up short, steep, and soft bank (3+). Continue on rail bed/Fish Lake Trail heading southwest.

2.9 Cross private access road.

3.9 Rock cuts. Start to climb gentle grade.

7.4 Cross under high concrete bridge and county road. Elevation 2,090 feet.

8.1+ Proceed through rail tunnel.

8.3 Cross dirt county road. County road just to north is Scribner.

8.7 Grade levels, enter open meadow space.

9.1 Come to wetland/northern end of Queen Lucas Lake. Waterfowl habitat here, basalt cliffs. Elevation 2,430 feet.

10.1 Merge with active rail line. Caution!

10.2 Cross right over active rail line. Caution! Then bear left immediately across open space and onto dirt access road.

10.4 Resume old rail line through basalt rock cuts.

11.0 Cross active rail line right. Caution! Proceed through stiles and into paved parking area/trailhead with plastic potties. The northern end of Fish Lake is visible ahead. A public beach and picnic area are accessed via a road to the right and down. To get to the turnaround point for this ride, though, go left on the paved trail that continues southwest and slightly uphill to the other end of Fish Lake.

11.5 Turn around here at the southern end of the lake and where the big pines start up again. Remember, though, that Cheney and Eastern Washington University are less than 4 miles farther on if you'd like a little longer cruise. Elevation 2,500 feet. Prosser Hill is across the lake and northwest of here.

12.0 Head back through stiles, across live tracks (Caution!), and then left back the way you came.

12.8 Cross live tracks (Caution!) and bear left.

14.9 Go through tunnel.

15.6 Go under high bridge.

19.0 Loose gravel, rocky.

20.0 Cross bridge.

20.4 Go down bank left, cross county road, and continue past STATE LAND sign back onto trail.

21.5 Cross Thorpe Road bridge.

22.4 Go left off rail line (Fish Lake Trail) and through Lindeke intersection.

22.5 Head uphill on 13th Avenue (paved) and under railroad bridge.

22.6 13th Avenue turns into Rosamond Avenue. Cross over Rosamond Avenue bridge.

22.7 Turn left on Woodland Boulevard and follow Woodland back to Finch Arboretum at 23.1 miles.

Centennial Trail West

Location: 5 miles west of downtown Spokane on the Spokane River.

Distance: 15.5-mile loop.

Time: 75–90 minutes.

Tread: Pavement.

Aerobic level: Moderate.

Technical difficulty: 1.

Hazards: Motor traffic, other bikes, and various foot traffic.

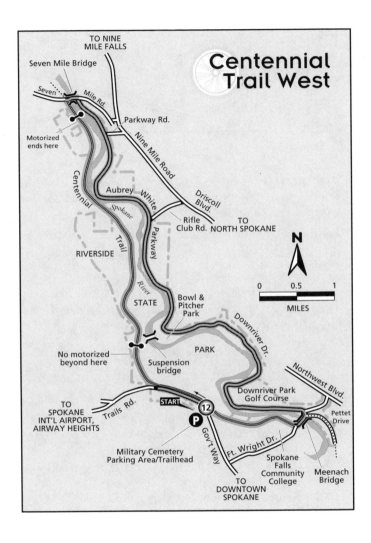

Centennial Trail West

TO NINE MILE FALLS

Seven Mile Bridge

Seven Mile Rd

Parkway Rd.

Motorized ends here

Nine Mile Road

Centennial Trail

Aubrey

White Parkway

Spokane

Driscoll Blvd.

Rifle Club Rd.

TO NORTH SPOKANE

RIVERSIDE

River

STATE

Bowl & Pitcher Park

Downriver Dr.

No motorized beyond here

Suspension bridge

PARK

Downriver Park Golf Course

Northwest Blvd.

TO SPOKANE INT'L AIRPORT, AIRWAY HEIGHTS

Trails Rd.

START

12

P

Gov't Way

Ft. Wright Dr.

Pettet Drive

Military Cemetery Parking Area/Trailhead

Spokane Falls Community College

Meenach Bridge

TO DOWNTOWN SPOKANE

N

0   0.5   1

MILES

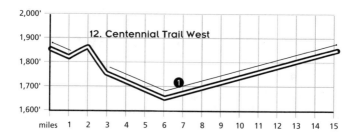

Highlights: Great views of the river, and access to Bowl and Pitcher Park and Riverside State Park. Depending on weather, can be ridden at least three seasons.

Land status: Public—dedicated pathway and city streets.

Maps: USGS Spokane NW, any good Spokane city map.

Access: 5 miles west of downtown, turn east off Government Way where Houston Road intersects from the west. The ride begins and ends at the Fort Wright Military Cemetery parking lot/trailhead on the Centennial Trail.

The Ride

0.0 Start from the east stiles of the Military Cemetery trailhead on the Centennial Trail (also called Riverside Park Drive or Aubrey White Parkway). Trail leads west through parking area.

0.1 Pass around metal gate, which leads to pathway. Begin small descent.

0.3 S turns are a lot of fun. Begin small climb.

0.4 View of river at small crest.

0.9 Small crest and then glide.

1.3 Another small crest.

1.4+ Smooth pavement meets rougher pavement. Go right and uphill. This is Aubrey White Parkway (and still the Centennial Trail). Watch for motor vehicles on this part.

1.5 Equestrian trails (closed to bikes) and stables are to right; stay straight ahead and climb moderate hill.

1.7 Crest and glide.

2.1 Views of river. Elevation 1,770 feet. Trees open up.

2.2+ Enter Bowl and Pitcher Overlook parking and cul-de-sac (motor vehicle access ends here). Go to far end (north) of parking area and go left around access gate.

2.4 Pass metal gate and old stone house on left. Big basalt escarpment to west.

2.5 Descend curves.

3.1 Cruise through rolling pines as you enter a burn area.

3.8 Begin medium grade climb.

4.0 Grade crests and levels.

4.1 Smooth gravel doubletrack heads left, singletrack goes right. Stay to main trail.

4.9 Pass flagpole—Civilian Conservation Corps site.

5.1 Descend small hill.

5.2 Come to Wilbur Road trailhead; pass through stiles. Watch for motor vehicles now as trees open up.

5.9 At Seven Mile Road go right across Seven Mile Bridge (Spokane River).

6.1 Go right immediately after crossing bridge, through stiles, and onto paved path, which leads to the eastern portion of Aubrey White Parkway. Now follow the east side of the river heading back south, with residences on left.

6.2 Climb gently and enter trees again.

6.7+ Bear right at Y in pavement.

7.0+ Enter Riverside State Park.

7.2 Descend hill above campground area.

8.5 Bear right as pavement smooths. Pass Spokane Rifle Club.

9.2 Begin moderate climb; it crests in a quarter mile.

10.2 Bowl and Pitcher Park and Riverside State Park headquarters are on right. Stay left to continue ride.

11.1 Begin passing sewage treatment facility, which continues for the next half mile.

12.1 Cruise and glide, and then climb briefly.

12.3 Stay right on pavement.

13.5 Begin climb to approach Meenach Bridge.

13.7 Go left at Y.

13.8 Go right at stop sign and onto bike lane that crosses the Meenach Bridge. Caution here: autos on bridge tend to fly!

14.1 Just after crossing bridge, go right down ramp to Centennial Trail. Go left on dedicated pathway and into trees again.

14.2+ Begin moderate climb.

14.5 Hill goes steep.

15.2 Trees open up. Views to northeast.

15.5 Complete loop at Fort Wright Military Cemetery trailhead.

Minehaha Loop

Location: Northeast of downtown Spokane.

Distance: 6.2 miles.

Time: 45–60 minutes.

Tread: 2 miles pavement, 1 mile doubletrack, 3.2 miles singletrack.

Aerobic level: Moderate.

Technical difficulty: 4-.

Hazards: Traffic on Upriver Drive, Frederick Avenue; soft spots and granite bedrock off road.

Highlights: Moderate climbing (about 500 vertical feet) with a wide variety of technical difficulties, some of the best singletrack in the area. We all owe a thank-you to the designer of this trail, a true gem.

Land status: Public and private.

Maps: Any good city map; USGS Spokane NE.

Access: From Argonne Road or Greene Street, get on Upriver Drive just north of the Spokane River. Shields Park is on the north side of Upriver Drive just upstream from Upriver Dam. Parking and potties are available there. The ride begins and ends at the Shields Park parking lot.

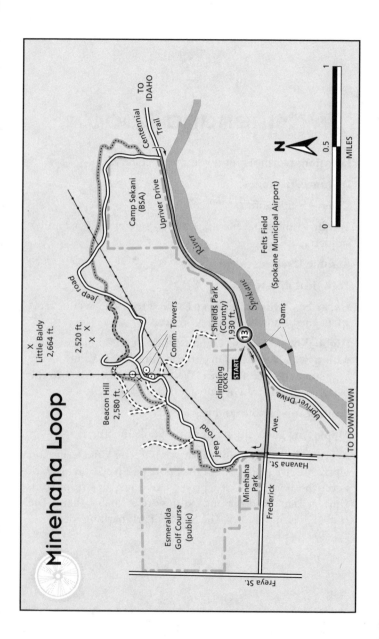

Minehaha Loop

× Little Baldy 2,664 ft.

2,520 ft. × ×

jeep road

Beacon Hill 2,580 ft.

Comm. Towers

Camp Sekani (BSA)

Upriver Drive

Centennial Trail

TO IDAHO

climbing rocks

Shields Park (County) 1,930 ft.

START

13

Dams

Spokane River

Felts Field (Spokane Municipal Airport)

Upriver Drive

TO DOWNTOWN

jeep road

Havana St.

Minehaha Park

Frederick

Esmeralda Golf Course (public)

Freya St.

N

MILES

0   0.5   1

The Ride

0.0 Start from Shields Park ("Minehaha Rocks" to local climbers) parking lot. Pedal west on Upriver Drive; its smooth pavement features a marked bike lane. Elevation 1,930 feet.

0.3 Bear right onto Frederick Avenue where Upriver Drive goes left to follow the river. Caution! Frederick is flat and busy. This section is best avoided during rush hours.

1.0 Go right on Havana Street (leaving pavement for gravel) and up a quick, steep grade at first entrance to Minehaha Park. Don't go left into park; stay on Havana, which deteriorates quickly.

1.2+ Follow a service road left, just before mile 1.2, as it winds around the upper side of Minehaha Park, still climbing, but now on a broken surface. Elevation 1,980 feet. Then go through steel gate. Just beyond at fork, stay to main road, bearing left.

1.3 Climb steep bedrock at saddle (2+).

1.4 On small ridge now, go straight ahead, bearing slightly right (toward Esmeralda Golf Course in the

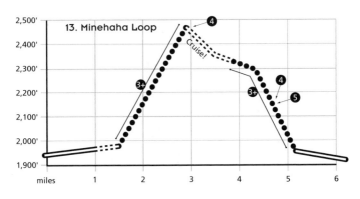

background). This will lead you onto a new single-track and avoid the fall-line grunt road that ascends the ridge to the right. Enter pines. Trail immediately begins to snake and wind, and calls for your full attention. It's a 3 and up for the next 1.5 miles.

1.8 Climb short, steep slope, then cross forest road up a steep, winding singletrack.

2.0- Grade mellows.

2.1 Switchback.

2.3+ Cross rocky service road, and keep to singletrack, proceeding through clearing and saddle. Elevation 2,200 feet.

2.4+ Drop briefly, cross road, staying to singletrack as you resume climbing.

2.6- Negotiate sharp switchback in small ridge clearing. Stay to singletrack as you cross jeep roads.

2.9 Climb steep, then it's flat as trail winds.

3.0 Come to clearing near top of Beacon Hill (aka Baldy); communications facilities are just ahead and left. Head northeast to far communication towers, bearing somewhat left. Proceed to road between two fenced-off facilities (about 25 feet apart) passing under power lines (2). Elevation 2,480 feet.

3.1 Go down second doubletrack to the right as you regain the trees. The first right is a very rocky track (mostly bedrock). This also follows a rocky fall line (4-).

3.2+ After some steep bedrock (4), grade continues down steeply, but surface is more benign; smooth rollers. Then bear left onto sandy doubletrack in clearing. (There's also a new singletrack heading southeast, for future reference.)

3.3 Cruise smooth (2).

3.5 Come out to wide gully under power lines.

3.6 Descend into gulch bottom, following this smooth, wide track.

3.7 Go through a double compression dip (3), then climb.

3.8 Go right on forest road just before mile 3.8. Hit a triple dip (sandy) this time; trail narrows. Cross creek bottom (there may or may not be water) and bear right onto a singletrack (3).

4.0- Trail goes sidehill right here, grassy. Fun rollers for the next little bit!

4.2 Climb up a short, winding, steep section.

4.3 Crest and swoop. Elevation 2,300 feet.

4.5+ Come to a ridge and compression dips.

4.7 Snake around screaming hairpins; very technical (4). Jumps and tight rocks push this section to 5; most will want to walk the worst (best?) sections.

4.9 Trail difficulty reasserts itself (4+).

5.0+ Cross jeep road, descend fall line right.

5.1 Go right on Upriver Drive. There's a bike lane here, but watch out! Pavement resumes. Elevation 1,960 feet.

5.2 Cross left over Upriver Drive and continue west on the Centennial Trail pathway that skirts the river.

6.2 Cross back over Upriver Drive to complete loop at Shields Park.

Marshall Dips

Location: 7 miles southwest of Spokane.

Distance: 8.2 miles, out and back.

Time: 50–60 minutes.

Tread: 7.6 miles dirt singletrack, 0.6 mile doubletrack and forest road.

Aerobic level: Moderate.

Technical difficulty: 3+.

Hazards: The most dangerous part of the entire ride is crossing Grove Road at the start and end; cars come whipping around this broad curve of pavement like it's a freeway! Other normal hazards are what make this ride unique: big roller coaster plunges and complementary climbs. Ruts, soft spots, and occasional rocky sections will teach you the finer points of using your front brake. The outer reaches of this ride hug the edge of a 60-foot bank, so beware of some exposure. Most of the dips are clearly visible, regarding traffic, from the tops. But timing is everything; you don't want to be cresting at a high rate while your mirror image is doing the same.

Highlights: Plunging, climbing, zooming—that's this ride in a nutshell. Most of the trail is soft dirt and smooth rolling. Your good friend, inertia, may turn against you, though. Exercise caution here; that potential energy you're carrying through the compression part of the wave may bite you.

Land status: Washington Water Power land. It's open to bikes, horses, and hikers and closed to motorized vehicles and hunters. Please be aware that this public access is a privilege granted by the utility company and, if abused, may be revoked.

Maps: Road map of Spokane County; USGS Spokane SW.

Access: From Spokane take Interstate 90 west to U.S. Highway 195 south. Take the Cheney-Spokane Road right off US 195 about 2 miles south of I–90 (at the gas station with a Tidyman's supermarket behind). Go about 5 miles on the Cheney-Spokane Road and turn right on Grove Road. Grove winds up a steep, curving hill. About a third of a mile past its junction with Andrus Road on a straight-away, stop at a county gravel pit on the west side of Grove Road. This pit is located at the top of a rise about a half mile north of the town of Marshall and the Cheney-Spokane Road. There's a wide spot in front of the pit. Please do not block the gate, and make sure that where you park does not restrict the gravel truck drivers' vision or ability to turn. The ride starts and ends about 100 yards back to the south at a silver gate/stile to the east side of Grove Road. A Washington Water Power sign warns NO MOTORIZED.

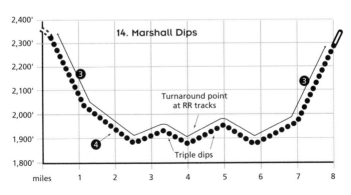

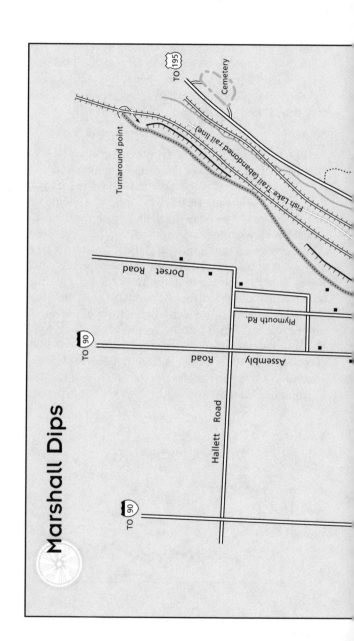

Marshall Dips

TO 90
TO 90
TO 195

Hallett Road
Assembly Road
Plymouth Rd.
Dorset Road
Fish Lake Trail (abandoned rail line)
Turnaround point
Cemetery

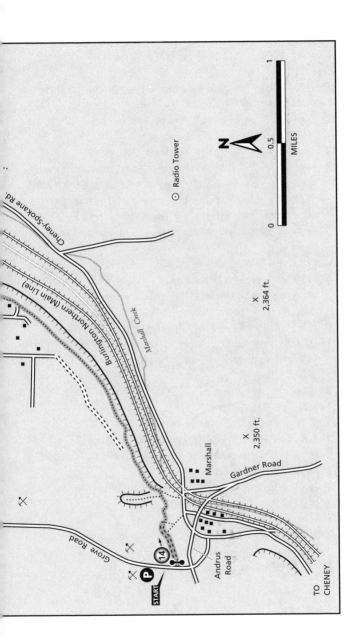

The Ride

0.0 Pass through gate/stile on Grove Road. Follow a faint, dirt doubletrack as it bears left and winds around flat through grass and pines. Elevation 2,370 feet.

0.2 Bear left at indefinite Y, mostly smooth.

0.3 Merge left with larger forest road from right. Single-track begins here. The forest road splits here into varied tracks, but they all diverge and converge over the next half mile. Our route (and mileage) will reflect the left-most singletrack. Trail here is smooth and wide.

0.6 Dip and cruise, curve.

0.8 Proceed straight through small gully (3-). (An intersecting singletrack follows the gully; it's a steep access trail from Marshall.)

1.0 Dip, rollers. From this point, the ride is mostly 3.

1.1+ Come close to edge of embankment—exposed. The Cheney-Spokane Road is visible here. Elevation 2,040 feet.

1.3- Double dips, banked rollers!

1.4+ Plunge down steep (3+)!

1.5 Enter a meadow and burn area.

1.5–1.8 Series of dips, rollers, and 3+ bumps.

1.9 Big, steep dip; watch out for ruts and soft spots (4).

2.2 Banked dips, rollers.

2.6 Descend close to railroad tracks, bottom out at 1,870 feet.

2.7 Dips!

3.0 Climb a bit. Cross fall-line ruts from gearheads destroying the embankment.

3.1+ Embankment ruts again. Exposed here.

3.3+ Pass rope-from-a-tree spot. Watch for kids playing, bikes lying in the trail, and Tarzan-like projectiles. Elevation 1,930 feet.

3.5–3.6 Triple dips (4-)!

3.9- Take fork right as track splits sidehill in a grassy area (1,920 feet).

4.1- Descend to Burlington Northern railroad tracks. Turn around and double back here. Elevation 1,880 feet.

4.7 Watch for exposed edge.

6.3+ Climb sustained hill.

6.8 Big dip!

8.2 Complete ride at Grove Road. How do your stomach muscles feel?

Garden Springs

Location: Southwest Spokane.

Distance: 6.2 miles.

Time: 30–45 minutes.

Tread: 2.8 miles pavement; 1 mile doubletrack/rail bed; 2.4 miles singletrack.

Aerobic level: Moderate.

Technical difficulty: 3.

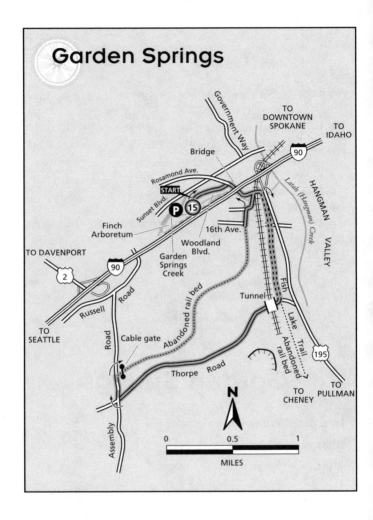

Hazards: Soft gravel; small, tight trees in short sections. These hazards should be eliminated in the near future as this old rail bed receives funding and an upgraded surface.

Highlights: Close in, but rural, this ride offers a wonderful variety of surface and terrain.

Land status: City and county, plus a section of private; please be aware of and obey trail closures and restrictions.

Maps: USGS Spokane SW; road map of Spokane County.

Access: The ride begins and ends at the Finch Arboretum (a Spokane city park) located west of downtown Spokane. To get there, proceed west on Second Avenue to Sunset Boulevard, turn left at Finch Arboretum, marked by a sign about a half mile uphill and after crossing Government Way. Follow Woodland Boulevard around to the right where the arboretum's main building and parking area are located.

The Ride

0.0 Start from the Finch Arboretum main parking area, just south of the main arboretum building. Head out parking lot and turn left on F Street (paved). Elevation 2,080 feet.

0.1 Wind around right and down as F Street turns into Woodland Boulevard.

0.4 Turn right on Rosamond Avenue and cross Interstate 90 over Rosamond bridge. Cruise down wide pavement as it winds left.

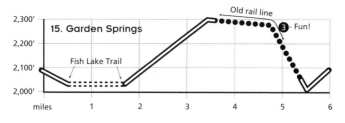

0.6 Cross under railroad bridge, then cross Lindeke Street at four-way stop. Proceeding straight ahead through this intersection (past DEAD END sign), leave pavement onto dirt; this is the north end of the Fish Lake Trail.

0.7 Go right on gravel rail bed. There are some earth berms (to keep motorheads out) that must be negotiated before the trail smooths out (2+).

0.9+ Cross 16th Avenue bridge (concrete and steel). Exercise caution here as the rock ballast is very loose.

1.2 Pass through basalt rock cut/escarpment. There is presently a large rock fall here that constricts the trail to a narrow, rocky slot. Elevation 2,000 feet.

1.3 Visual boundaries open up as trail proceeds on levee.

1.5 Just before crossing the Thorpe Road bridge, go right and down steep embankment (4). At bottom, bear right through meadow and toward cyclone fence opening.

1.6 Go left through fence, over green barrier gate, and then right up pavement, climbing a gentle grade, which is Thorpe Road. Elevation 1,980 feet. Proceed through tunnel; exercise caution!

2.2 Grade increases to moderate.

3.2 Turn right off Thorpe and onto Assembly Road. Grade eases and begins to crown. Elevation 2,300 feet.

3.3 Bear right off Assembly, past cable, and onto an old, abandoned rail bed. It's now little more than a smooth section of wide singletrack, mostly level.

3.5 Trail narrows to singletrack.

4.1 Cross under power line. There's a nice view here out over Hangman Valley.

4.5- Come to a rocky, occasionally wet area. Trees/undergrowth close in; caution here.

4.8 Go right down a split in the trail. This short, rocky, and technical section leads down and away from the rail bed and an old bridge site over a basalt gully to your left.

4.9 Go right at split, through fun curves (3), then cross and rejoin trail that went straight at split.

5.1+ Cross rocky jeep road. Stay on singletrack; it merges left onto hard-packed doubletrack, which quickly changes to hard-packed singletrack. This is a short but great trail with the rail bed off to the right a safe 50 feet (and down maybe 40 feet).

5.2+ Trail splits slightly up and left into open, and slightly down and right into trees. Go right and into trees.

5.4+ Singletrack ends at pavement, 14th Avenue. Proceed right on 14th and under railroad bridge with 11-foot-8-inch clearance marked. Go left on Lindeke and down hill.

5.5+ Turn left on 13th Avenue and pass under railroad bridge.

5.8 Turn left on Woodland Boulevard and follow Woodland back to Finch Arboretum at 6.2 miles.

High Drive
Parkway North

Location: Lower South Hill in Spokane on the very western edge above Latah (Hangman) Creek.

Distance: 4.8-mile loop.

Time: 30–40 minutes.

Tread: 2.5 miles dirt/singletrack, 2.3 miles paved (city streets).

Aerobic level: Easy.

Technical difficulty: 3 mostly with 4 sections, some exposure! Not for the timid.

Hazards: Exposure over steep embankments; rocky, narrow, and steep singletrack.

Highlights: Great views over Hangman Valley; for the skilled rider, this ride is a lot of fun but not easy. It also presents another way into the High Drive Parkway trails system without entering and finishing from the top.

Land status: Spokane city park land and some private (about the first mile of the ride). At present, this access and the start of this trail are open to the public through the good nature of local landowners. Be aware of any changes in access status, and obey all signs. This is one of those areas where behavior and etiquette of trail users will determine whether or not future use continues.

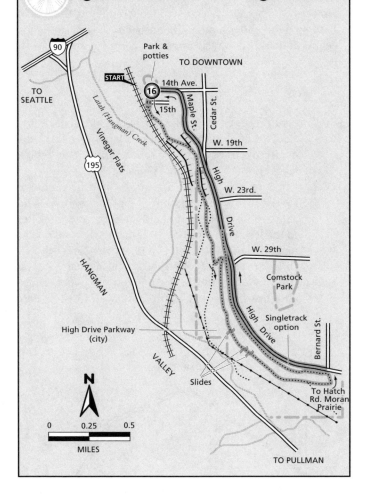

High Drive Parkway North

Park & potties

TO DOWNTOWN

START

14th Ave.

16

15th

Maple St.

Cedar St.

TO SEATTLE

Latah (Hangman) Creek

Vinegar Flats

W. 19th

High Drive

W. 23rd.

W. 29th

HANGMAN

Comstock Park

High Drive Parkway (city)

High Drive

Singletrack option

Bernard St.

VALLEY

Slides

To Hatch Rd. Moran Prairie

N

TO PULLMAN

0   0.25   0.5

MILES

Maps: Any good Spokane city map; USGS Spokane NW and Spokane SW.

Access: From downtown Spokane, go south on Maple Street and turn right (west) on 14th Avenue. At the end of 14th is a neighborhood park on a cul-de-sac. The ride begins and ends here. Parking is available for a few cars.

The Ride

0.0 From the end of the 14th Avenue cul-de-sac (located at about ten o'clock as you drive in), head over broken ground on a sewer access road, which leads through some large pines.

0.1 Cross by end of 15th Avenue, which drops down steeply from left, where railroad access road and gate are to the right and a posted fence corner lies to the left. Pass around this fence corner and onto a dirt singletrack. A steep and narrow gravity well (big dip) awaits. It's also rocky. This is really a good entrance exam for this ride; if you can't safely negotiate this first obstacle, you may want to abort here (4-).

0.3 Climb into pines.

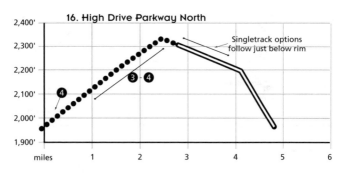

0.4 Grade turns steep and becomes exposed on right bank.

0.5 Crest and glide momentarily in a grassy area.

0.6 Trail splits; either fork is okay as they rejoin shortly. Beware, though, the right track goes thin and is close to an exposed edge.

0.8 Forks rejoin.

0.9- Trail splits again. Take right one. Track then drops through a rocky dip (4)! Take middle track as two tracks split into three.

1.1 Trails cross here again; go left at split and continue up on south-running track.

1.2 Negotiate a rocky dip (3) and climb a narrow track.

1.3+ Rocky dip (4, this time).

1.4+ Come to a T/switchback via a steep, short pump. Go left and climb a serious and soft grade (4-). We're now heading momentarily north. Elevation 2,220 feet.

1.5+ Take sharp switchback right and up (4). Here is the test of this ride. The grade eases after a short bit, and you head back south.

1.6 Crest and glide after rocky 4. Trail mellows amid scattered pines.

1.7 Gun a short spurt up a tricky 3+ sidehill.

2.0 Pump for another quick rise, then cross (carry over) a slide.

2.3- Glide though a basalt-lined gully (3+) and gingerly pick your way through fall-line ruts.

2.4 Go left and up at Y switchback. Down and right is access to further undeveloped city park land, bordered by Latah Creek and Qualchan Golf Course (city). Climb moderately steep hill.

2.5 Go left as you reach the top of the High Drive Parkway at Bernard Street. Elevation 2,360 feet. You're right at the edge of where the city meets an escarpment dropping 500 feet at a 50 percent grade. You now have the choice of following a dirt/gravel singletrack immediately left that hugs the forest rim or the High Drive itself (a wide, paved, residential connector with marked bike lanes). Either way, go left (north), and watch for lots of foot and auto traffic.

2.7 Option: Another singletrack drops down into the dirt; it follows your route and is more technical.

3.0- Lower singletrack merges back with High Drive.

3.5 Go left where High Drive meets 29th Avenue coming in from the right.

3.6 Between the rim and High Drive is a small parking pullout. Option: Another dirt singletrack drops from the north side of the pullout area, by some concrete steps.

3.8 Singletrack from 3.6 merges back with High Drive at small sidewalk alcove.

4.2 Grade begins to increase down. High Drive turns into Cedar Street. Just after that, go left onto Maple Street. Watch for high-speed urban fliers! Cruise, checking your own tendency to fly.

4.6 Go left on 14th Avenue and down steep hill.

4.8 Complete loop back at park.

High Drive Parkway

Location: The extreme west boundary of the South Hill in Spokane.

Distance: 5.3-mile loop.

Time: 35–45 minutes.

Tread: 0.5 miles forest road/doubletrack, 4.8 miles single-track.

Aerobic level: Moderate.

Technical difficulty: 2–4.

Hazards: Other trail users; steeps, soft, and narrow trail in places; some exposure, rocks.

Highlights: This ride requires advanced bike skills and a climb out at the end, but for those who relish the more difficult end of the spectrum, this loop is a classic. Views and terrain are superlative.

Land status: City park land.

Maps: Any good city map; USGS Spokane SW.

Access: On High Drive, just west of Bernard Street, there's limited parking (six or so spaces) and an unmarked trail-head on the South Hill rim. Get there from Maple Street or U.S. Highway 195 and Hatch Road, or on 57th Avenue coming from the east. High Drive can also be reached by Grand Boulevard from downtown. The ride begins and ends at the parking pullout on High Drive.

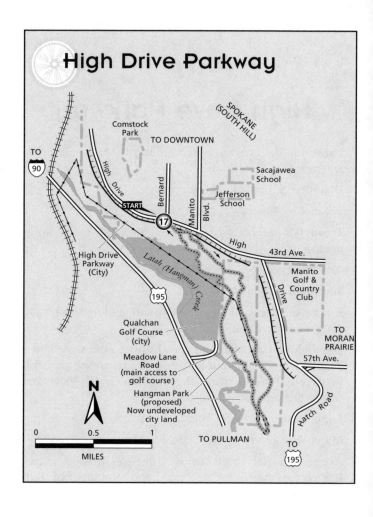

High Drive Parkway

Comstock
Park

TO DOWNTOWN

SPOKANE
(SOUTH HILL)

TO
90

High Drive

START

17

Bernard

Manito

Manito Blvd.

Jefferson
School

Sacajawea
School

High

43rd Ave.

High Drive
Parkway
(City)

Latah (Hangman) Creek

195

Manito
Golf &
Country
Club

Manito Drive

TO
MORAN
PRAIRIE

Qualchan
Golf Course
(city)

57th Ave.

Meadow Lane
Road
(main access to
golf course)

Hangman Park
(proposed)
Now undeveloped
city land

Hatch Road

N

0   0.5   1

MILES

TO PULLMAN

TO
195

The Ride

0.0 At the parking pullout on High Drive about 50 yards south of Bernard Street, go down a south-running singletrack that descends from the rim. Elevation 2,400 feet.

0.3- Negotiate an S turn and switchbacks.

0.4 Descend through dips under a canopy of pines.

0.5 Go through tight turns (3). Fun!

0.7 Scream through a gravity well (big dip), preferably with your mouth closed. Climb a short, moderate hill immediately after.

0.8 Crest on small ridge.

1.0- Come to a T at a ridgetop, then swoop and grind out of it, bearing left. Elevation 2,250 feet.

1.1 Climb a sustained steep-to-moderate hill, and traverse clearing.

1.3 Crest and drop through pines.

1.4 Swooping rollers! Descend!

1.6 Stay left to main track; a singletrack heads off right. Wonderful roller coaster continues down.

1.7 Swoop to power lines and clearing.

2.0 Bear left on forest road, descending gently now.

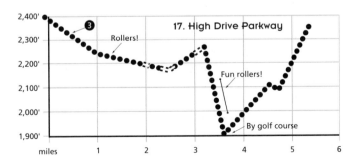

2.1 Go through a sweeping right-hand turn, then go left on singletrack into thick trees and away from meadow road. It's now flat cruising.

2.5 Come to utility access road near the bottom of Highland Park Drive. Loop around to the left on a singletrack and backtrack. Elevation 2,160 feet.

2.7+ Go right and up on singletrack.

2.9+ Go left on doubletrack, climbing sidehill.

3.1 Grade levels. Elevation 2,280 feet.

3.2 Doubletrack is smooth; go left under power lines, and climb moderate increasing grade.

3.4 Follow trail around a sharp left turn as you crest and enter rollers, leaving power lines. Trail narrows slightly to wide singletrack.

3.5–3.9 This section of trail is excellent for its smooth rollers and banked turns!

3.9 Bottom out just a few yards from the Qualchan Golf Course. Elevation 1,910 feet.

4.0 Follow trail as it narrows further and heads through an S turn and up a steep hill.

4.2 Gain small ridgetop through a series of turns. Then go right to stay on a steepening, rocky ridge. (A singletrack goes left here.)

4.3 Gain a rocky knob and go left, diving briefly and joining the route by which you came.

4.5 Swoop through curves.

4.6 At fork go right and up.

4.9 Continue right and up moderate, rocky grade where a thin singletrack comes in from left.

5.0 Climb through an S turn and a pair of switchbacks.

5.1 Switchback right goes to Manito Boulevard; stay left.

5.2 Grade mellows; pump final steep section and complete loop at 5.3 miles.

Spokane Valley

Centennial Trail East

Location: Spokane and east to Spokane Valley 10 miles.

Distance: 22.2 miles, out and back.

Time: 90–120 minutes.

Tread: Almost completely paved.

Aerobic level: Moderate.

Technical difficulty: 1.

Hazards: Auto traffic crossing roadways and foot traffic everywhere on Upriver Drive.

Highlights: Following the Spokane River most of the route; transition between urban and wild environments. Great training ride in off-hours; very social at peak hours. Kiosks at trailheads with posted YOU ARE HERE markers.

Land status: Public, dedicated trail, city, and county streets.

Maps: Centennial Trail map; any good city, metro, or valley area map; USGS Greenacres, Spokane NE, Spokane NW.

Access: From Trent Avenue, just east of Division Street and then north on Riverpoint Boulevard, or from Gonzaga University campus via Hamilton Street. The Don Kardong–Burlington Northern Bridge, where the ride begins and

Centennial Trail East

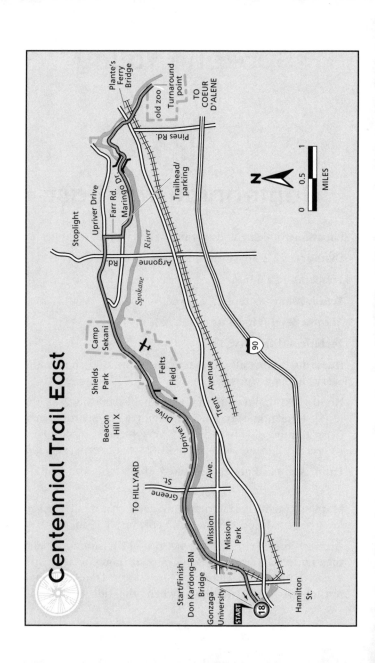

ends, connects Gonzaga and SIRTI (Spokane Inter-collegiate Research and Technology Institute) campuses over the Spokane River.

The Ride

0.0 Starting from the middle of the Don Kardong–BN Bridge, head northeast (toward Gonzaga). A very colorful structure, the bridge has sideouts (small wider sections) with tables. On flat pavement (Centennial Trail), pass the Gonzaga athletic complex on left. Elevation 1,850 feet.

0.2 Cross Hamilton Street via concrete footbridge.

0.3 Cross service road.

0.4 Cross street at stop sign.

0.8 Pass Mission Park on left. Stay to paved pathway at east end of park.

0.9 Go right at Mission Avenue. Cross railroad tracks. Caution! This is a busy area.

1.0 Cross Mission, turning left, and head up Upriver Drive. Caution! Upriver Drive has a wide bike lane.

2.4 Cross under Greene Street Bridge.

4.0 Turnout sections of the Centennial Trail for the next 2 miles are protected by stiles. In these sections it's best for bikes to stay to the bike lanes by the road. Upriver Dams are on the right. There's a drinking fountain here on the trail by a bench.

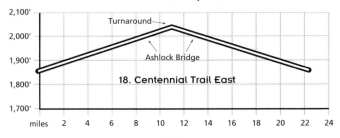

4.2 Go right at stop sign. Frederick goes left while Upriver Drive continues right.

4.6 Pass Shields Park on the opposite side of Upriver Drive; this is the local urban rock-climbing area (known as Minehaha Rocks). Potties there. Grade climbs gently.

5.7 Pass Boulder Beach trailhead on the Spokane River to right, a natural rocky point.

6.1 Enter higher-density residential area; shoulder narrows briefly. Caution! Elevation 1,950 feet.

7.0 Cross Argonne Road through a stoplight, one of only two on the Centennial Trail in Spokane. Caution! Traffic is usually heavy here. Continue on Upriver Drive straight ahead.

7.4- Go right and descend slightly at Farr Road. You're still on a designated bike lane.

7.8- Go left at Maringo Drive.

7.9 At dead end of Maringo, enter cul-de-sac and trailhead. Proceed right through stiles to gain paved pathway. You're now in grassy meadowland and entering a more natural environment. Ponderosa pines shield a natural estuary. Over the course of the next mile or so, singletracks veer off randomly here and there.

8.7 Look up to your left above the rimrock and you'll see the Riblet mansion.

9.0 Cross the Spokane River via a concrete footbridge (Ashlock Bridge), only this one's big enough to drive a tank over. Another trailhead is just to the left before the bridge; potties are available there.

9.3 Pass an especially scenic, sandy boulder area. Large basalt columns have made a unique spot on the river here.

9.5 Cruise through S turns.

9.6 Climb short, moderate hill.

10.1 Cross under Trent Avenue bridge. Remains of Plante's Ferry Bridge are just beyond.

10.3- Cross under railroad bridge.

10.8- Pass trailhead on right.

11.0 Pass through rock cuts in trail; potty just beyond. Cross small footbridge.

11.1 Come to Walk-in-the-Wilds Zoo kiosk. The zoo is not here anymore, but this is an interesting place to poke around; remnants and trails can be found if you look. Elevation 2,050 feet. When you're ready, turn around and head back the way you came.

12.1 Pass back under Trent Avenue bridge.

13.1 Cross over river and then left.

14.3 At trailhead go left and onto Maringo Drive.

14.5 Go right and up Farr Road.

14.9 Go left onto Upriver Drive.

15.2 Cross Argonne Road.

17.9 Bear left and stay on Upriver Drive.

21.2 Go right on Mission Avenue, over railroad tracks, and then left at Mission Park.

21.8 Cross two streets, staying to pathway.

21.9 Cross Hamilton Street bridge, then cross service road.

22.2 Complete ride at Don Kardong–BN Bridge.

State Line Loop

Location: The Idaho-Washington state line at Interstate 90.

Distance: 12.8 miles.

Time: 60–90 minutes.

Tread: Paved nonmotorized trail and roads.

Aerobic level: Moderate.

Technical difficulty: 1.

Hazards: Other trail users, crossings, and traffic.

Highlights: This is a great training or road ride. Up one side of the Spokane River in the flats and back the other via the foothills of Mica Peak, this ride is a good introduction to the opportunities between Liberty Lake, Washington, and Post Falls, Idaho.

Land status: Public rights of way.

Maps: USGS Liberty Lake, Washington; Post Falls, Idaho.

Access: From I–90 near the Idaho-Washington line, take exit 299 in Washington; it's also the state port of entry and a rest area with visitor information, so there's plenty of parking and potties. The ride begins and ends at the entrance stile (at the chain-link fence) between the rest area and the Centennial Trail.

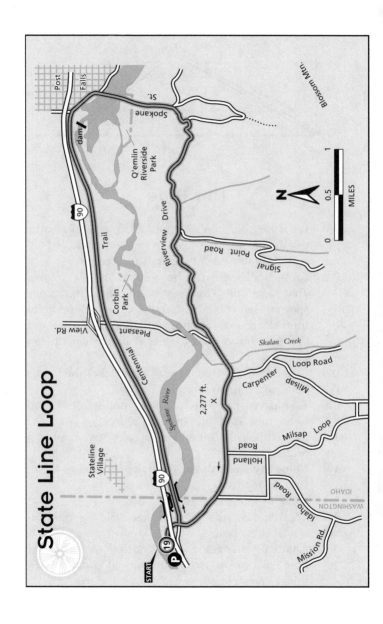

State Line Loop

Stateline Village

Post Falls

dam

Q'emlin Riverside Park

Spokane St.

Blossom Mtn.

Signal Point Road

Riverview Drive

Corbin Park

View Rd.

Centennial Trail

Pleasant

Spokane River

2,277 ft. X

Skalan Creek

Carpenter Loop Road

Milsap

Holland Road

Milsap Loop

Idaho Road

Mission Rd.

WASHINGTON IDAHO

START

P 19

90

N

0   0.5   1

MILES

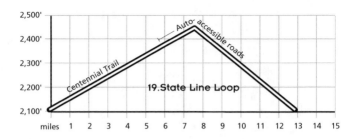

2,500'
2,400'
2,300'
2,200'
2,100'

Auto- accessible roads

Centennial Trail

19.State Line Loop

miles 1 2 3 4 5 6 7 8 9 10 11 12 13 14 15

The Ride

0.0 Pedal east on the Centennial Trail just behind the rest area facilities. You're on the north side of I–90 and the south side of the Spokane River.

0.2 Cross Spokane Street to resume the Centennial Trail. Caution! This may be the most hazardous spot on the whole loop; traffic comes whipping in from off the freeway (from left), and there are about four other directions to watch! Remember this on your way back.

0.5 Cross under I–90 as the trail approaches the river.

0.7 Idaho state line trailhead is on right.

0.8 Take paved pathway fork left, continuing east on Centennial Trail. Elevation 2,120 feet.

1.0 Cross Spokane River via an old steel-span rail bridge.

1.4 Come to a small rise as the trail gets close to I–90.

1.9 Pass through stiles.

3.1 Cross Pleasant View Road.

3.2, 3.7, 3.9, 4.3 Cross paved roads. Yield the right-of-way at these points.

5.1 Climb a gentle grade as rocks define the canyon at Post Falls to the right (south). Old concrete arch bridge (now closed) is visible over the river.

5.5 Pass through stile on Centennial Trail.

5.7 Centennial Trail leads to an arterial in Post Falls. Cross arterial (Second Street) as pathway resumes through an open, grassy park area.

5.8 Turn right on Spokane Street, and then cross two sets of railroad tracks. Shasta Butte is directly ahead and to the south on horizon. At this point, you leave Centennial Trail; it goes off left and on to Coeur d'Alene.

6.1 Cross Spokane River on new concrete bridge. Old pilings and dam are visible to the right (west).

6.4 Just after you cross the river, turn right (over turf and down small hill) through Q'emlin (pronounced *kay MEE lin*) Riverside Park. This is a short detour; it's a great rest area or spot for lunch. Aside from the sandy beach for swimming, there are rest rooms, drinking water, phone, playgrounds, and even a rock-climbing area if you go to the far end of the park by the dam. For this ride (to keep your mileage straight), you're just pedaling over to the beach area and then back out through the parking lot.

6.5 Get back onto Spokane Street and continue proceeding south (the way you were going previously). Grade starts to rise.

6.8 Climbing moderate grade through a well-kept residential area, you enter an area of pine trees. Riverview Drive goes left; stay right on Spokane Street.

7.2 Sidewalk and residential area end. Begin climbing a serious grade through rock cuts. While you're pumping this monster, just consider this hill a big spring you're winding, and when you get to the top, you can unwind it.

7.5 Grade levels and drops. Elevation 2,450 feet (summit).

7.6 Curves here are made for bicycles. Zoomers!

8.5 Pass Signal Point Road on left (White Fence Vineyard, also). Stay on main road and get ready for the drop and cruise.

9.1 Thirty-mph curves here. If you're doing this on a bike, what's that Porsche doing coming the other way? Caution!

9.5 Madison Road (gravel, county) goes off right here; stay to main road.

9.8 Old schoolhouse on left.

10.0 Pleasant View Road makes a sharp right here (paved). Stay to main road.

10.1 Enter pines again.

10.3 Climb to Pleasantview Church.

10.7 Grade levels.

10.8 Grade drops quickly to flats in open meadows.

11.4 Holland Road goes left; stay to main road.

11.5 Reach bottom of flats.

11.9 Begin gentle drop.

12.3 Come to a curve with old farmhouse and line of maples on right. This now dumps into Spokane Street and junction of Appleway.

12.6 Proceed toward I–90 and cross under.

12.8 Complete loop at starting point/rest area back in Washington state.

Carpenter–Milsap Roads Loop

Location: Just east of the Washington-Idaho line and south of Interstate 90 and the Spokane River.

Distance: 6.8-mile loop.

Time: 40–55 minutes.

Tread: 5.2 miles dirt/gravel county road, 1.6 miles paved.

Aerobic level: Moderate.

Technical difficulty: 1+.

Hazards: Auto traffic, mostly on Riverview Drive, but be aware of driveways and drivers with styled hair and cell phones.

Highlights: Great views of Mica Peak (Idaho), east Spokane Valley, and the Rathdrum Prairie. This is a classic country road ride with enough vertical to give you a workout.

Land status: County roads.

Maps: Coeur d'Alene National Forest; USGS Post Falls, Idaho; any good Coeur d'Alene/Post Falls vicinity map.

Access: From Post Falls take Spokane Street over the Spokane River. Bearing right, it turns into Riverview Drive. Continue west about 4 miles to where Carpenter Road (the east end) meets Riverview. From the state line, take Washington exit (exit 299) on I–90, go under the freeway and

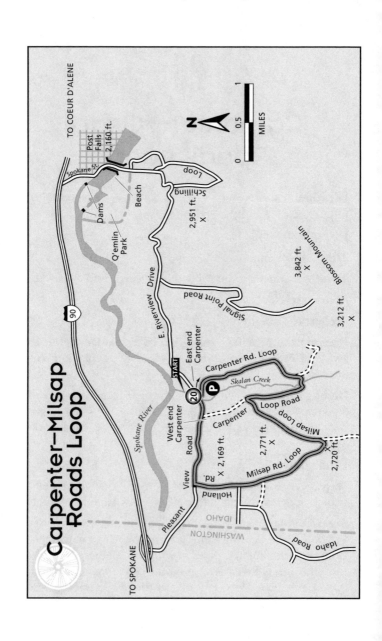

Carpenter–Milsap Roads Loop

TO SPOKANE

TO COEUR D'ALENE

Post Falls
2,160 ft.

Spokane St.

Dams

Beach

Q'emlin Park

Schilling Loop

2,951 ft. X

Blossom Mountain

3,842 ft. X

3,212 ft. X

Spokane River

90

E. Riverview Drive

Signal Point Road

START

20

East end Carpenter

P

Carpenter Rd. Loop

Skalan Creek

West end Carpenter Road

Loop Road

Milsap Loop Road

2,771 ft. X

2,720 ft. X

Milsap Rd. Loop

Pleasant View Rd.

Holland

X 2,169 ft.

WASHINGTON
IDAHO

Idaho Road

N

MILES
0   0.5   1

toward Idaho on the old Pleasant View Road, which turns into Riverview Drive. Follow this to the second (east) Carpenter Road junction. There's a cute, little white farmhouse and fence at that junction. Parking is limited and not advised on Riverview Drive. If you go up Carpenter 50 feet, there are spots for a few autos on the west side, next to the farm. The ride begins and ends at the east end of Carpenter Road Loop.

The Ride

0.0 Start up Carpenter Road (east end). It rises moderately with a gravel surface. Elevation 2,100 feet.

0.2 Shutter bumps. Climb steeply now.

0.5 S turns; limited visibility; caution! Climb steeply, again.

0.7 Vista to west; postcards, anyone?

1.3 Crest and begin descent. Views of Mica Peak to south. Elevation 2,520 feet.

1.4 Go right at split.

1.5 Plunge through gully bottom (2,470 feet).

1.8 Bear right to main road where Steinpreis Road comes in left. Negotiate S turns through forest now.

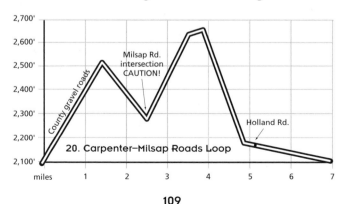

20. Carpenter–Milsap Roads Loop

2.3 Bottom out and then climb (2,250 feet).

2.6 Take a sharp left at the junction with Milsap Road Loop. Climb steep. Caution! Watch out for speeding cars and construction traffic.

3.0 Rise to another vista of Mica Peak.

3.4 Crest hill at a broad saddle (2,660 feet).

3.6 Rise a bit more to summit of this ride (2,680 feet).

3.8 Descend sweeping downhill section and sharp turn to right.

4.3 Go through a series of S turns and steep downhill ride.

4.8 Wind around a series of flattening curves (2,180 feet).

5.2 Go right at Holland Road (paved).

5.5 Rise up from meadow bottom and go right on West Riverview Drive (paved, aka Pleasant View Road).

5.9 Climb through an S turn as you leave meadow flats.

6.0 Pass Dominican Church to your right.

6.8 Complete loop at starting point.

Liberty Lake Loop

Location: Liberty Lake, 10 miles east of downtown Spokane, just west of the Idaho line.

Distance: 7.5-mile loop.

Time: 40–60 minutes.

Tread: 4.7 miles pavement, 1.5 miles gravel/dirt road, 1.3 miles singletrack.

Aerobic level: Moderate.

Technical difficulty: 2.

Hazards: Some soft/wet spots in the park meadows. Traffic: narrow, busy neighborhoods. Close to the lake, the town of Liberty Lake is congested, so be alert and courteous.

Highlights: Circumnavigating Liberty Lake is the point of this ride; this is perhaps the easiest way around the lake (on two wheels or less). Starting at the county park at the lake's southern end, you're in pristine meadow and woods. A rolling meadow trail is unsurpassed for surface and scenic enjoyment, rising and fading gracefully into the development that is now Liberty Lake, Washington.

Land status: Liberty Lake County Park, public roads and streets.

Maps: USGS Liberty Lake, Mica Peak, Washington; Spokane County road map.

Access: From Interstate 90 near the Idaho-Washington line, take the Liberty Lake exit onto Liberty Lake Road,

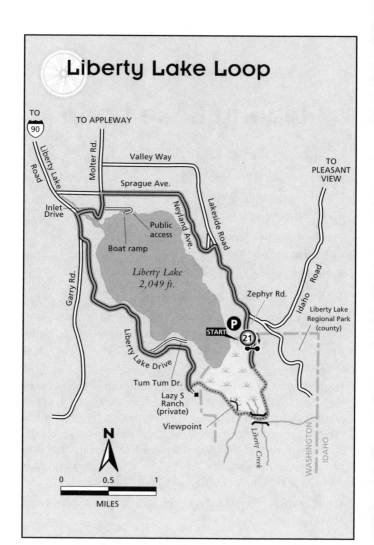

Liberty Lake Loop

TO [90]

TO APPLEWAY

Liberty Lake Road

Molter Rd.

Valley Way

Sprague Ave.

Inlet Drive

Neyland Ave.

Lakeside Road

TO PLEASANT VIEW

Idaho Road

Public access

Boat ramp

Garry Rd.

Liberty Lake 2,049 ft.

Zephyr Rd.

Liberty Lake Regional Park (county)

START P ⊕ 21

Liberty Lake Drive

Tum Tum Dr.

Lazy S Ranch (private)

Viewpoint

Liberty Creek

WASHINGTON IDAHO

N

0   0.5   1

MILES

heading south about 1.2 miles. Turn left at Sprague Avenue and follow it for about 1 mile. Bear right; follow Neyland Avenue. Neyland winds around the northeast side of Liberty Lake. Bear right at a junction with Lakeside Road; it's then another mile or so to Zephyr Road, where a county park sign directs you right to where it ends at the park. To the right and before the entrance gate is a small dirt parking lot. The ride begins and ends here. Park fees (less than $10 per vehicle per day) are required during the summer season.

The Ride

0.0 Start from the off-season parking lot before and to the right of the park entrance gate. Pedal on dirt/gravel road that takes you through the entry gate. Mostly level, the park road rises gently around a beautiful picnic area.

0.2+ Bear left at fork that takes you around the east side of the campground loop.

0.6 Turn left at trailhead map (a tall structure with a map protected by acrylic) and pass through gate. Trail turns to wide singletrack dirt that levels through mixed pines. Elevation 2,130 feet.

0.9 Turn right off main trail onto a dirt singletrack. You'll pass a wood-frame ropes structure.

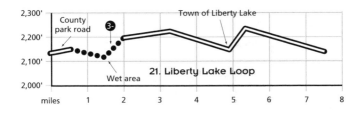

1.1 Go right at split (Edith Hanson Riding Trail is signed to the left here) and cross Liberty Creek over a small wood bridge.

1.4+ Climb gently to a rocky viewpoint of the lower Liberty Creek meadowland and refuge.

1.5 Swoop through a low area (can be wet half the year here) of wonderful, rolling singletrack.

1.8 Climb a steep, rocky, narrow trail with close brush (3).

1.9+ Come upon a gravel county road. Lazy S Ranch is to the left where the road dead-ends. Go right (north) here on mostly level peas and marbles.

2.1 Small crest.

2.5 Pass a wide parking shoulder on right.

2.8 Pavement begins. Go left onto Liberty Lake Drive. Tum Tum Drive goes right here.

3.1 Climb moderate hill.

3.6 Narrow residential area here, 20 mph!

4.3 Liberty Lake Road comes in from left here.

4.5 Go right on Inlet Drive.

4.7 Inlet Drive turns into Molter Road; follow it as it curves and climbs.

4.9 Go right on Sprague Avenue, a four-way stop.

5.0 Climb to a rise as you pass golf course on left.

5.1 Grade levels at 2,250 feet.

5.5 Drop down a zoomer! Beware the speed limit.

5.8 Climb winding curves.

6.3 Watch out for a sharp left in the road.

6.5 Bear right onto Lakeside Road where Neyland Avenue ends at Y.

6.6 Drop through some curves and then climb.

7.2 Go right and down Zephyr Road (marked by COUNTY PARK sign) and then down final zoomer to complete loop at 7.5 miles.

Liberty Creek Loop

Location: Liberty Lake County Park, about 10 miles east of downtown Spokane.

Distance: 8.9-mile loop.

Time: 90–120 minutes.

Tread: 1.2 miles park road/doubletrack, 7.7 miles single-track.

Aerobic level: Strenuous.

Technical difficulty: Ranging from 2 to 5, but mostly 4.

Hazards: Steep, narrow, and rocky singletrack; streams, soft spots, downed trees—you name it! This is an advanced ride, not for the timid.

Highlights: This challenging trail will be fun for those who are prepared for it. For those who aren't, this is not where to learn your trail skills. Lots of steep ups and downs, lots of getting on and off your bike, and a rocky, thick forest trail make this a sustained expert loop. There's even a waterfall or two. Connections to Mica Peak (Idaho) and beyond are the rewards for those who have the gas to get there.

Land status: Liberty Lake Regional (Spokane County) Park land.

Maps: USGS Liberty Lake, Mica Peak, Washington; Spokane County road map.

Access: From Interstate 90 near the Idaho-Washington line, take the Liberty Lake exit onto Liberty Lake Road, heading south about 1.2 miles. Turn left at Sprague Avenue

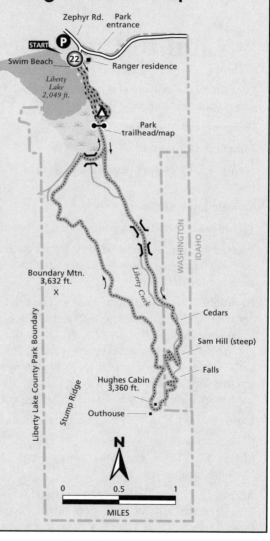

Liberty Creek Loop

Zephyr Rd.

Park entrance

START

P

22

Swim Beach

Ranger residence

Liberty Lake 2,049 ft.

Park trailhead/map

WASHINGTON

IDAHO

Boundary Mtn. 3,632 ft.
X

Liberty Creek

Cedars

Sam Hill (steep)

Falls

Hughes Cabin 3,360 ft.

Liberty Lake County Park Boundary

Stump Ridge

Outhouse

N

0   0.5   1

MILES

and follow it for about 1 mile. Bear right; follow Neyland Avenue. Neyland winds around the northeast side of Liberty Lake. Bear right at a junction with Lakeside Road; it's then another mile or so to Zephyr Road, where a county park sign directs you right to where it ends at the park. To the right and before the entrance gate, there is a small dirt parking lot. The ride begins and ends here. Park fees ($10 per vehicle per day) are required for the summer season.

The Ride

0.0 Start from the off-season parking lot before and to the right of the park entrance gate. Pedal on dirt that turns into a gravel road that takes you through the entry gate. Mostly level, the park road rises gently around a beautiful picnic area.

0.25 Bear left at fork that takes you around the east side of the campground loop.

0.6 Turn left at trailhead map (a tall structure with a map protected by acrylic) and pass through gate. Trail turns to wide singletrack dirt that levels through mixed pines. Elevation 2,130 feet.

1.0 Stay to main trail left in grassy meadow area. Singletrack also goes right.

1.5 Begin moderate climb after passing through small meadows.

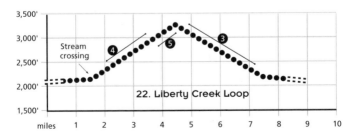

1.6 Cross Liberty Creek. This is a rocky and hazardous crossing; even if you're a trials rider, carry your bike on this one to keep the bank erosion to a minimum.

1.7 Climb a rocky section here (2).

2.1 Difficulty goes to 4+; big, sharp rocks.

2.45 Cross small wood bridge and creek again; carry bike over a short steep hump.

2.7 Come to cedar grove; trail then goes right up Sam Hill. Get ready for this series of steep switchbacks, which must be pushed and carried through (5).

3.1 Grade eases; trail goes narrow and sidehill. Elevation 2,860 feet.

3.3 Difficulty gets serious again (4).

3.6 Gets even worse! (5) Steep and thin. Elevation 2,940 feet.

3.7 Exposed sidehill; steep and short descent into cedared gully, cross wood bridge with 30-foot waterfall on right. Follow trail up steep switchback that winds around and above waterfall, following creek. Watch for windfall and narrow spots here.

4.3 Cross small wood bridge over creek in cedars; grade mellows out. Then, at a forest road junction, go straight ahead on a dirt singletrack and up a short hill. This is an important junction: The left leads up to Mica Peak and huge potential for future biking, and the right leads directly down to the park from where you came. It's also marked by a sign I have never encountered before. It reads: MORE BIKING. It's living proof that park managers have wit. After climbing a short hill, this singletrack winds through thick second growth and just right of an outhouse built to service the Hughes Cabin. This is the summit of this ride. Elevation 3,360 feet.

4.4 Following this singletrack down a bit leads to the Hughes Cabin, a primitive structure put up by Boy

Scouts. This is a good bivouac spot; it has a wood-stove and bunks. See the park manager about use guidelines and reservations if you're interested. From the cabin, follow a wide singletrack down and left in a westerly direction. This is a smooth section of old forest road.

4.5 Merge left with road coming in from right; this is where the MORE BIKING junction road comes in from. Caution for the rest of this ride: This trail section, all the way to the park, is designated for horses and other nonmotorized uses. Keep your speed in check! The steepness of this downhill is more serious than it seems at first, when allowing for the many soft spots, ruts, and loose rock.

4.8 Cross creek.

5.1 Rocky sidehill: It's 3, rocky, and soft.

5.5 Cross a wet seep (spring).

6.6 Scenic trail goes left; stay right and down to main trail, soft sand here.

6.8 Ruts! (3)

6.9+ Scenic trail goes left; stay right and down main trail again.

7.1 Steep downhill, humps.

7.3–7.4 Rolling 3, rocky, ruts.

7.6 Pass through wood gate; grade and surface mellow.

7.7 Pass sign for the Edith Hanson Riding Trail (faces downhill). Meadow area begins. Go about 50 yards and then bear right on main trail.

7.8 Cross wood bridge over Liberty Creek.

7.9+ Trail forks; either way will lead you back to the main trail.

8.0 Bear left at main trail by which you came.

8.3 Come back to main trailhead sign; go left at campground gravel road.

8.9 Complete loop back at park gate.

Idaho and Vicinity

Mount Spokane–
Mount Kit Carson

Location: Mount Spokane State Park, about 15 (air) miles northeast of Spokane.

Distance: 10.6-mile loop.

Time: 90–120 minutes.

Tread: 5.6 miles pavement, 1.3 miles forest road/doubletrack, 3.7 miles singletrack.

Aerobic level: Moderate to strenuous.

Technical difficulty: Singletrack 2–4.

Hazards: Other bikers, horses, and hikers. On the Mount Kit Carson Loop Road lower end, watch for picnickers and stroller-running mamas. The climb up State Route 206 is steep, narrow-shouldered, and heavily trafficked at times. With all the inherent, self-inflicted dangers of the downhill, the climb up is by far the greatest hazard of this ride.

Highlights: The excitement of this loop is obviously the downhill. While you grind up in the sun, the swoop is almost completely protected by a canopy of deep forest.

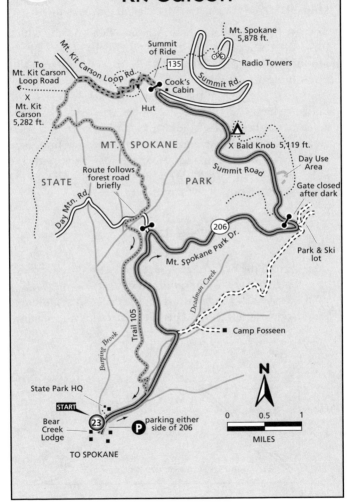

Mount Spokane–Mount Kit Carson

To Mt. Kit Carson Loop Road

Mt. Kit Carson Loop Rd.

Summit of Ride

135

Mt. Spokane 5,878 ft.

Radio Towers

Cook's Cabin

Summit Rd.

Hut

X Mt. Kit Carson 5,282 ft.

MT. SPOKANE

STATE

Route follows forest road briefly

PARK

X Bald Knob 5,119 ft.

Summit Road

Day Use Area

Gate closed after dark

Day Mtn. Rd.

206

Mt. Spokane Park Dr.

Park & Ski lot

Deadman Creek

Burping Brook

Trail 105

Camp Fosseen

State Park HQ

START

23

parking either side of 206

Bear Creek Lodge

P

TO SPOKANE

N

0   0.5   1

MILES

Cedars, hemlocks, and firs play backdrop over a forest loam floor and track. What is the range of your experience?

Land status: Mount Spokane State Park.

Maps: USGS Mt. Spokane, Mt. Kit Carson, Washington.

Access: From Spokane, take Argonne Road north (which turns into Bruce Road past Bigelow Gulch). Turn right at Mount Spokane Park Drive (State Route 206); a sign at this point indicates it's 13 miles to Mount Spokane State Park from here. Just before the entry to the park is Bear Creek Lodge, where the ride begins and ends. Aside from the amenities of hot meals, cold drinks, and the like, the operators have offered bike and rider shuttle service from here and may or may not continue to do so. Check with the lodge for current info, (509) 238–9114. Pull into parking areas on either side of the pavement.

The Ride

0.0 From the Bear Creek Lodge, pedal up the pavement, a gentle grade. Elevation 3,000 feet.

0.3 Pass park headquarters and maintenance buildings on your left. Note: This is the place for information, rescue, fees, etc. Climb moderate grade.

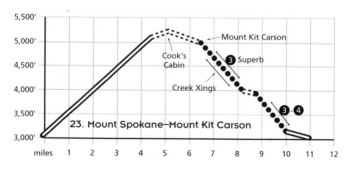

0.5 Trail 105 is marked and drops down from the left; you'll be coming back that way.

1.1–1.6 Climb through a series of steep switchbacks.

2.0 The lower end of the Mount Kit Carson Loop Road is to the left. The descent will take you a short distance from here. Continue climbing the pavement at this hairpin.

2.4–2.5 Climb steep and winding.

3.2 Stay to paved road left (Mount Spokane Park Drive), climbing. Pavement to the right is Ski Lodge Road. Note that the gate here is closed after dark in the summer.

4.1 Vista left.

4.3 Pass Day Use Area and Bald Knob Campground to the right. Elevation 5,119 feet.

4.8 Grade mellows.

5.1 Go left off pavement, through gate, and onto upper end of Mount Kit Carson Loop Road. It's a wide, level forest road in thinning trees. At 5,240 feet, it is the summit of this ride.

5.2 Trail 135 intersects here. This leads down off the top of Mount Spokane by the radio towers. Stay to main track; smooth cruising.

6.2+ Descend through steep, rocky curves (3). Go left at dirt singletrack. There's a potty here; just right is a wider track that ascends over Mount Kit Carson. This is where the fun begins; most of the remainder of this ride is a singletrack dance. Take a moment. Run a field check before you let gravity take you away. And remember, horses especially don't like silent, swift surprises. Consider everything 3 minimum until you get back to the pavement.

6.5 Negotiate a series of tight S curves.

6.7 Trail narrows as logs frame both sides of trail.

6.8 Track goes narrow with roots and rocks (4-).

7.0 Cross small brook, surrounded by mountain alders.

7.1 Cross another smaller (seasonal) brook. Watch for punji stakes as trail widens briefly.

7.4 Enter bumpy, rocky section.

7.5–7.6+ Cross seasonal brook. At 7.6, bear left where singletrack merges with our trail from the right; it comes down from Mount Kit Carson.

7.8 Drop through a wet draw (gully) and seep (spring) as trail flattens and smooths.

8.0 Cross Burping Brook over a corduroy (log) bridge (4). Elevation 4,040 feet. Just a bit farther on, a singletrack drops down from the left; it comes from the Bald Knob campground. Stay right to main track.

8.1 Go right onto smooth forest road in deep cedars; this is the lower end of the Day Mountain Loop Road. Watch for grannies and *Sunset Magazine* photographers. Cross over Burping Brook again and through picnic area.

8.3 Take smooth singletrack left and onto Trail 105, off of forest road at hairpin curve. Zoom down rolling trail, crossing another creek.

9.1 Bottom and climb out of draw as the trail widens. For the next half mile, the trail climbs and dips through meadows and forest.

9.7 Negotiate steep S curves with ruts (4). Pass under power lines.

9.9 Descend through a series of three tight switchbacks (4).

10.0 Descend steep, narrow, and somewhat exposed trail over fixed and loose rock (4+). Also, watch for hikers coming up the trail.

10.0+ Go right at the pavement (Mount Spokane Park Drive) the way you came up. Watch for traffic!

10.3 Pass park headquarters to your right.

10.6 Complete loop back at Bear Creek Lodge. And don't forget to check out the lodge upstairs, where good food and a rustic atmosphere can be found.

Mount Spokane–Linder Ridge

Location: Mount Spokane State Park, about 15 (air) miles northeast of Spokane.

Distance: 6.6-mile loop.

Time: 30–60 minutes.

Tread: All forest road/doubletrack.

Aerobic level: Easy.

Technical difficulty: 2–3.

Hazards: Other bikers and hikers.

Highlights: This short, easy route is mostly cruising and a good introduction to the Mount Spokane area. Because it starts at 4,600 feet, it's also a good spot to escape the summer heat down in the valley. This loop follows the Nordic ski trail system, so it's well marked and offers a minimum of climbing.

Land status: Mount Spokane State Park, Inland Empire Paper Co.

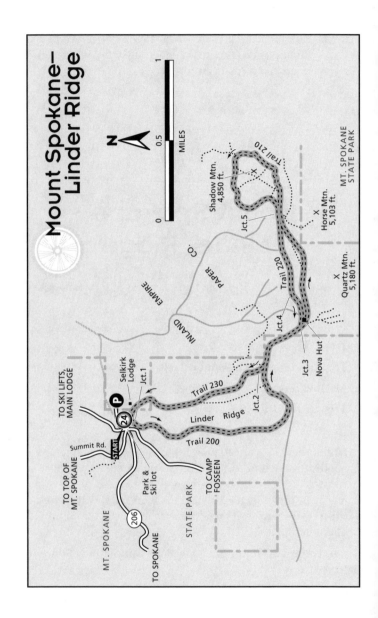

Mount Spokane—Linder Ridge

MILES

N

MT. SPOKANE STATE PARK

Shadow Mtn. 4,850 ft.

Trail 210

Jct. 5

X Horse Mtn. 5,103 ft.

INLAND EMPIRE PAPER CO.

Trail 220

X Quartz Mtn. 5,180 ft.

Jct. 4

Jct. 3

Nova Hut

Trail 230

Selkirk Lodge

Jct. 1

P

24

TO SKI LIFTS, MAIN LODGE

Jct. 2

Linder   Ridge

Trail 200

Summit Rd.

START

TO TOP OF MT. SPOKANE

Park & Ski lot

206

MT. SPOKANE

TO SPOKANE

STATE PARK

TO CAMP FOSSEEN

Maps: Mount Spokane State Park Nordic trail system map; USGS Mt. Spokane, Mt. Kit Carson, Washington.

Access: From Spokane, take Argonne Road north (which turns into Bruce Road past Bigelow Gulch). Turn right at Mount Spokane Park Drive (State Route 206); a sign at this point indicates it's 13 miles to Mount Spokane State Park from here. From the park entrance, past Bear Creek Lodge and park headquarters, go another 3 miles to a large gravel pullout on the right; this is the Snow Park parking lot. Go right here another two-tenths to the Selkirk Lodge Nordic hut (open in winter) and parking area. The ride starts and ends right in front of the Selkirk Lodge.

The Ride

0.0 From the Selkirk Lodge, head south across the parking lot. Elevation 4,600 feet.

0.1 Climb up over a dirt embankment with a trail signboard just beyond. Take Trail 200, which is slightly left. It's flat to rolling, soft and mostly smooth doubletrack, and in the trees.

0.4 Vista to west.

0.5 At Junction 1 (all junction and trail numbers are Nordic trail designations), which is a big opening in

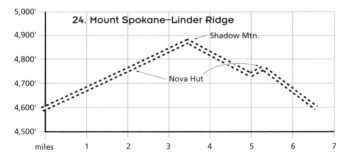

127

the woods and saddle, go straight ahead and slightly right (south), keeping to Trail 200. You're on Linder Ridge now. Cruise and dip a bit.

0.8   Bottom out, crest a small hill, and cruise.

1.1   Crest and cruise some more.

1.3- Shoot through a hollow and wind through some fun curves.

1.4+ Come to Junction 2 in a saddle; go right, keeping to Trail 200.

2.0   Climb short steep hill (3). Elevation 4,740 feet.

2.1   Come to Nova Hut at Junction 3. Go left just past the hut, and then in about 100 feet, go right (south) onto a smooth quartz-gravel forest road.

2.9   Drop moderately through some fun rollers.

3.0+ Come to Junction 5 (complete with potty; you'll pass Junction 4 on the return). Continue on the main track heading east. Option: Right near the potty, there's a singletrack that leads to the top of Horse Mountain. It's not far but can be rugged.

3.1   Bear left onto Trail 210 to Shadow Mountain, climbing moderately.

3.2   Crest hill as a singletrack drops in from the left.

3.3   In a saddle, a vista opens up southeast.

3.7   Climb up to a saddle where the trail Ts; you're on Shadow Mountain now and the top of this ride at 4,850 feet. Numerous signs indicate that this is the juncture of the Nordic trail and the bubbleheads' (snowmobilers) domain. Bear left on a doubletrack that heads around the north side of Shadow Mountain; a Nordic trail sign (skier pictograph) is posted to the right.

3.8   Drop and level out, then go right at T.

4.3   Stay to main trail, bearing right at Y, dropping moderately.

4.4 Stay right to main track, then go left back to Junction 5.

4.4+ Go right on Trail 220. After a short bit, traverse a wet bog; it's best to carry your bike around the uphill side of this (3+). Trail gets somewhat rugged.

4.5 Doubletrack gets overgrown, and then goes to rolling.

5.0 Merge with larger trail at bottom of moderate hill; this is Junction 4. Now bear left and uphill, climbing through mile 5.1.

5.2 Proceed right on main smooth track; you're about 100 yards east of the Nova Hut and Junction 3, the way you came in. This is still Trail 220.

5.6- Go right at Junction 2 onto Trail 230; this is a fun section of swooping and cruising (2+).

6.2 Back at Junction 1, bear right to stay on Trail 230. Wind through open forest road to complete loop back at Selkirk Lodge at 6.6 miles.

Coeur d'Alene: Centennial Trail East

Location: From Coeur d'Alene to Blue Creek Bay along the edge of Lake Coeur d'Alene.

Distance: 14.4 miles out and back.

Time: 1–2 hours.

Tread: Pavement; most of it is a dedicated bike/pedestrian trail.

Aerobic level: Moderate.

Technical difficulty: 1.

Hazards: Watch out for places where autos cross the Centennial Trail, and of course, there's always street traffic in Coeur d'Alene.

Highlights: This out-and-back follows Lake Coeur d'Alene's northeastern shore and serves as this community's athletic promenade. It's well protected as a dedicated path; there are also plenty of potties on the way at the numerous Parking Lot Observation Sites, which usually consist of auto parking, potties, picnic tables, and historic markers.

Land status: Public right-of-way.

Maps: North Idaho Centennial Trail and Municipal Parks (Coeur d'Alene Parks Department), any good Coeur d'Alene city map, USGS Coeur d'Alene, Fernan Lake, Idaho.

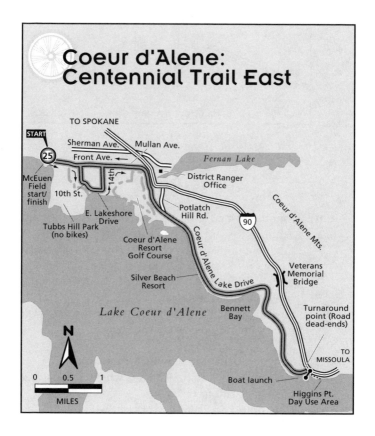

Coeur d'Alene: Centennial Trail East

TO SPOKANE

START

25

Sherman Ave.

Mullan Ave.

Front Ave.

Fernan Lake

McEuen Field start/ finish

10th St.

14th

District Ranger Office

E. Lakeshore Drive

Potlatch Hill Rd.

Coeur d'Alene Mts.

Tubbs Hill Park (no bikes)

90

Coeur d'Alene Resort Golf Course

Silver Beach Resort

Coeur d'Alene Lake Drive

Veterans Memorial Bridge

Lake Coeur d'Alene

Bennett Bay

Turnaround point (Road dead-ends)

N

TO MISSOULA

0   0.5   1

Boat launch

MILES

Higgins Pt. Day Use Area

Access: In downtown Coeur d'Alene, this ride begins and ends at the McEuen Field Complex and city parking lot located on Front Avenue just east of the Coeur d'Alene Resort. The city offers free parking (you need to punch in and out at an attended gate) for the first two hours at this large lot.

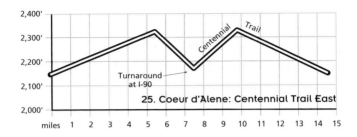

25. Coeur d'Alene: Centennial Trail East

The Ride

0.0 From the east edge of the city parking lot on Front Avenue (in front of the City Parks Department Building and just west of the tennis courts), pedal east on Front Avenue. A wide section of sidewalk in front of the tennis courts is dedicated Centennial Trail. Elevation 2,160 feet.

0.2- Merge right onto Mullan Avenue, passing City Hall on the right. Follow BIKE TRAIL signs.

0.4 Go left on Pine Street.

0.5+ Go right on 10th Street, which curves around.

0.6- Merge into Mountain Avenue, which snakes and hugs Tubbs Hill to the right.

0.7+ Come onto East Lakeshore Drive, winding around and passing a marina.

0.9- This quaint neighborhood is defined by its mansions and lakeshore gazebos.

1.0+ Follow the pavement as it makes a sharp left at the front gate of Jewett House.

1.1 Go left on Ash Street, then right on 14th Street.

1.3- Go left on Lost Avenue, then right up a short hill, and back onto 14th Street.

1.5- Go right onto Mullan Avenue; now you're back on the main Centennial Trail route.

1.9 Pass a cemetery to your left and the Coeur d'Alene Resort Golf Course to your right.

2.1- Go right on Coeur d'Alene Lake Drive. Caution: This is the old main highway, and it's still a multilane arterial at this point. Watch for traffic!

2.2 Climb a gentle grade on a wide, dedicated shoulder/bike lane. Interstate 90 is just north and above you.

2.8 Crest and pass under Potlatch Hill Road.

2.9 Pass a Centennial Trail monument/marker at a Parking Lot Observation Site.

3.2 Pass by the Silver Beach Resort to the right. Caution! This is a busy marina, and the right-of-way is theirs.

4.0 Parking Lot Observation Site.

4.7 Parking Lot Observation Site. This one has a monument describing the Veterans Memorial Bridge that towers hundreds of feet above you, completing one of the most dramatic spans of the new I–90.

4.9 Watch out for autos accessing a resort, then climb a big, sweeping curve.

5.4 Pass and yield to Bennett Bay Resort traffic.

5.5 Crest hill and begin smooth glide. You just climbed 200 feet over the last half mile.

5.7 Yellowstone Trail Road goes off left. Stay to present route.

5.9 Booth Park Road goes off right. Stay to present route. Watch for traffic.

6.0 Cruise down moderate grade.

6.5 Parking Lot Observation Site.

6.8 Parking Lot Observation Site and climb slightly through rock cuts.

7.3 Boat launch and Parking Lot Observation Site to right.

7.6 Come to end of Centennial Trail where I–90 traverses before you. At the gate/stile through a cyclone fence is your turnaround point. If you want to go a bit further, pass through the fence and check out Higgins Point Day Use Area at the end of the path. This route now goes back the way you came.

9.1 Crest hill.

9.7 Crest and glide.

12.4 Potlatch Hill crest.

13.1 Go left at Mullan Avenue.

13.9 Cross 11th Street and yield.

14.2 Pass City Hall to your left, then go left onto dedicated sidewalk/trail.

14.4 Complete loop at starting point.

Canfield: Cave Trail Loop

Location: Northeast of Coeur d'Alene, Idaho, at the western edge of the Coeur d'Alene Mountains.

Distance: 7.2-mile loop.

Time: 60–75 minutes.

Tread: 1.6 miles paved, 4.2 miles gravel/dirt forest road, 1.4 miles singletrack.

Aerobic level: Moderate.

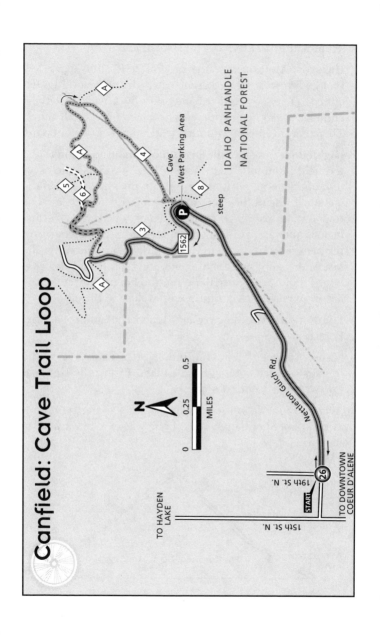

Canfield: Cave Trail Loop

N

0   0.25   0.5
MILES

TO HAYDEN LAKE

15th St. N.

START

19th St. N.

26

TO DOWNTOWN COEUR D'ALENE

Nettleton Gulch Rd.

IDAHO PANHANDLE NATIONAL FOREST

West Parking Area

Cave

P

1562

steep

8

3

4

5

6

A

Technical difficulty: 2–4 on singletrack.

Hazards: Motorized traffic on Forest Road 1562, a few rocky, narrow, or steep sections of singletrack (nothing sustained). This area is used intensely by a wide variety of enthusiasts, so keep your eyes and ears open at all times. There may even be a wounded wild animal or two out here.

Highlights: Consider this short loop an introduction to the Canfield Mountain Trail System. Like the singletrack section of this loop, most of the trails in the system are on the technical side of the spectrum. Familiarity helps a lot. The trail system map is an excellent color topo in small scale; major junctions are posted on site and are referenced on the map. This trail system should also be recognized for the rare and highly successful community effort that has coalesced motorheads, pedalers, and the Forest Service to create an intensely used multiuse area close to the city.

Land status: City, county, and Idaho Panhandle National Forest.

Maps: Canfield Mountain Trail System (available at the Fernan District Forest Office), Idaho Panhandle National Forest; USGS Coeur d'Alene.

Access: From downtown Coeur d'Alene, go north on 15th Street off of Sherman Avenue. Follow 15th about 2.2 miles

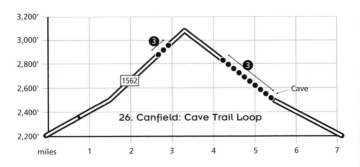

to Nettleton Gulch Road. Go east about 0.3 mile to where 19th Street meets Nettleton Gulch Road. The ride begins and ends at this T intersection. There's limited parking in this well-shaded neighborhood.

The Ride

0.0 Pedal east on Nettleton Gulch Road. It starts out paved and flat through a residential area and scattered pines. Elevation 2,200 feet.

0.3 Climb gently, leaving residential area.

0.8 Pavement ends. Climb gravel on gentle to moderate grade.

1.3 Pass wide turnout on left; climb steep grade as road narrows; surface degrades (3-). Watch for downhill traffic!

1.7 This is the west parking area for the Canfield Trail System. You're now on FR 1562; follow it up left and steep. Singletracks funnel in from north and east. Elevation 2,530 feet.

2.6 Go right on Trail A. This is a wide singletrack in clay soil that crosses over a large ditch and then some big kelly humps. Note that this turnoff may or may not be marked, and it may look different due to storm damage and logging.

2.7 Wide singletrack winds sidehill and east; cross fall-line trail with humps and dips (3).

2.9 Stay to Trail A as it turns north at a junction marked with a map. Trail 3 is to your extreme left as it winds up a ridge and falls away to the right; A is now forest road. Elevation 3,000 feet. Climb gentle to moderate grade.

3.2 Reach the top of this ride (3,150 feet) as Trail 6 splits off left and up. Stay right to A.

3.7 Trail 5 drops down from the left.

3.9 Descend into a draw (gully).

4.0 Grade drops more seriously.

4.2 Hit a dip and climb again.

4.3 Trail narrows to singletrack in forest opening, lush undergrowth around. From this point on, the fun begins: rolling, banked turns surrounded by a canopy of green. This is solid 3 with some tricks that will land you on your ear if you're not paying attention.

4.5 Roots, treewell (4).

4.6 Go right on Trail 4 (Cave Trail) where it splits as it meets a creek bottom. Trail A continues left and crosses the creek.

4.9 Roots (4).

5.2 Trail makes a detour of its old route as it rises briefly and shoots through a narrow, rutted section (3+).

5.4 Descend through a switchback left, steep, exposed (4)! Another 50 feet down and just before a switchback right is an old cave and namesake of this trail. Check it out: It's 40 feet deep and cool, even when it's 90 degrees outside. After the second switchback, plunge down a rocky, winding trail.

5.5 Go left at the west parking lot where you picked up FR 1562. Cruise down the gravel (watch that steep section at the top) and pavement of Nettleton Gulch Road back to where you started at 7.2 miles.

27

Canfield Buttes Outer Loop

Location: Northeast of Coeur d'Alene, Idaho, at the western edge of the Coeur d'Alene Mountains.

Distance: 20.8 miles.

Time: 2–4 hours.

Tread: 10 miles paved, 10.8 miles gravel/dirt forest road.

Aerobic level: Strenuous.

Technical difficulty: 2.

Hazards: Motorized traffic on Forest Road 1562 (four-wheel-drives, ATVs, dirt bikes, you name it!), auto traffic on pavement, especially by Fernan Lake; narrow or no shoulders, tight and blind curves.

Highlights: If you can handle the hazards of this demanding loop, you're paid off with rugged mountain and lake views, pristine meadows, and an excellent introductory tour of the Canfield Mountain Trail System. Many of the singletrack trails in this complex intersect this access road, including access to both Canfield Butte summits.

Land status: City/county streets and Idaho Panhandle National Forest land.

Maps: Canfield Mountain Trail System (available at the Fernan District Forest Office), Idaho Panhandle National Forest; USGS Coeur d'Alene and Lane.

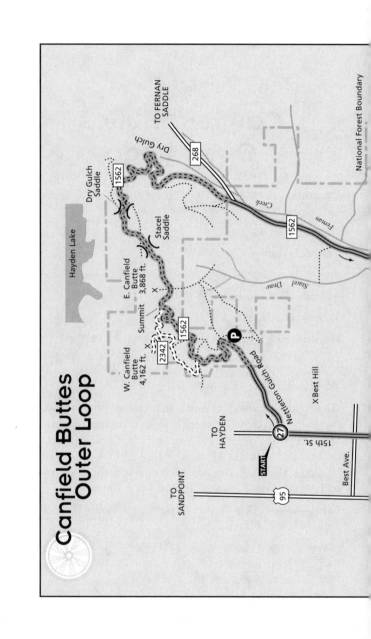

Canfield Buttes
Outer Loop

Hayden Lake

TO FERNAN SADDLE

Dry Gulch

1562

Dry Gulch Saddle

268

Stacel Saddle

1562

Fernan

Creek

National Forest Boundary

E. Canfield Butte 3,868 ft.

Summit X

W. Canfield Butte 4,162 ft.

Stacel Draw

1562

2342

Summit X

P

Netliateron Gulch Road

X Best Hill

TO HAYDEN

START

27

15th St.

X Best Hill

TO SANDPOINT

95

Best Ave.

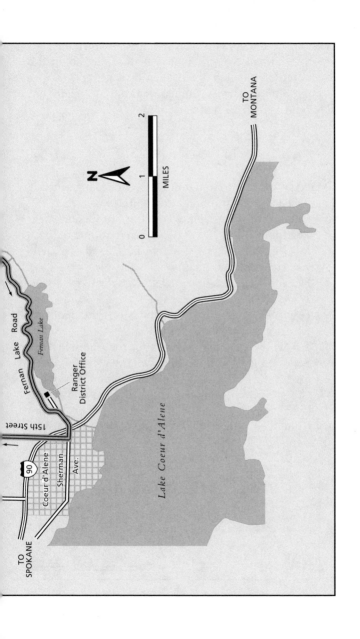

Access: From downtown Coeur d'Alene, go north on 15th Street off Sherman Avenue. Follow 15th Street about 2.2 miles to Nettleton Gulch Road. The ride starts and ends at this intersection. There's limited parking on Nettleton Gulch Road just off 15th Street.

The Ride

0.0 Pedal up (east) Nettleton Gulch Road. It starts out paved and flat through a residential area.

0.3 Climb gently, enter pines, and leave residential area.

0.8 Road rolls, dips, and curves. Watch out for traffic!

1.0 Road rises moderately. Maple Leaf Road goes left; stay right to main track.

1.3 Pavement ends. Climb gravel on gentle to moderate grade.

1.8 Pass wide turnout on left; climb steep grade as road narrows; surface degrades (2+).

2.3 This is the west parking area for the Canfield Trail System. FR 1562 starts here, what you'll be following for the bulk of this ride. Follow FR 1562 up left and steep. Singletracks funnel in from above and right.

2.6 Unmarked singletrack intersects from left. Continue on FR 1562.

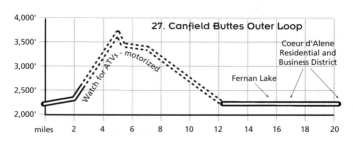

2.7 Road forks; stay right to main branch. Rocky surface and ruts here.

2.8 Bigger ruts.

3.1 Switchback goes steep briefly.

3.5 Trail A (singletrack) intersects FR 1562. Stay on FR 1562.

3.7 Stay to main road on right switchback.

4.0 Trails C and 3 intersect at wide spot here (parking for three cars, maybe). Gnarly nature of these intersecting trails gives you a good indication of the kind of riding you'll find in this area of the trail system. Stay on FR 1562.

4.6 Trail 6 intersects road. Stay on FR 1562.

5.1 This is the first summit of the ride (3,750 feet). Go right and down to stay on FR 1562 and this loop. FR 2342 goes left to West Canfield Butte (the higher of the two buttes in this area). Trails 2 and 5 also intersect at this point, and straight ahead and up a short rocky road is a viewpoint to Hayden Lake and the north. Continuing on FR 1562, grade drops steeply and then eases up.

5.4 Grade drops steeply again. Trail D intersects FR 1562 at what's known as the Island. Stay on FR 1562.

5.5 Begin gentle rise.

5.8 Trail 9 (Jump Trail) intersects road; taking it to the left (north) will lead you to the summit of East Canfield Butte. Continue on FR 1562 east and descend gently.

6.2 Leave forest canopy briefly; this is an open sidehill section, created by the fire of 1972. Descend gently.

6.7 Arrive at Stacel Saddle. Trails D and 10 intersect here; stay on FR 1562.

7.0 Rise gently; road curves.

7.5 Grade begins slight descent.

7.7 Stay to right and FR 1562; this is Dry Gulch Saddle. Trails 11 and 28 intersect. Road smooths, and views to south open up. Begin descending now.

8.6–8.7 Negotiate tight turns as you enter the trees. The remainder of this forest road offers some great soft/broken surface cruising; just be prepared for anything!

8.8–9.6 Hairpin turns.

9.7 Rise briefly.

9.9 Resume descent.

10.0 Begin a series of tight turns.

10.2–10.4 Hairpins over creeks.

10.6 Stay left to main road as a right fork leads to a gate and parking area. FR 1562 gets rocky and bumpy as it meets and follows a branch of Fernan Creek. Hemlocks and cedars now dominate the forest.

11.7 A cedar grove to the left provides shelter for an unimproved campsite near creek.

11.8 Draw opens up; surface changes to rocky shale.

12.1 Go right on Fernan Lake Road, which is paved. Narrow shoulder and year-round traffic, so caution is advised for this part of the ride especially. This area is a scenic wonder also, taking you through rolling meadows, quaint farms, and natural wetlands.

14.0 Bottom out; begin a slight rise.

15.1 This is the east end of Fernan Lake; the road hugs the northern rocky shore. It's rolling and scenic, but be aware of the tight and blind curves. This is a favorite local fishing spot.

17.4 Enter residential area.

17.8 Pass Fernan Ranger District Office on left. Information and potties are available here.

17.9 Fernan Lake Road turns into Sherman Avenue as you pass under Interstate 90. Caution is advised again as you enter a busy commercial district.

18.5 Turn right on 15th Street, heading north and climbing gently.

19.6 Cross under I–90 again.

20.5 Cross Best Avenue, a major arterial and stoplight.

20.8 Complete loop at Nettleton Gulch Road, where you started.

Mineral Ridge Loop

Location: About 10 miles southeast of Coeur d'Alene, overlooking Beauty Bay on Lake Coeur d'Alene.

Distance: 6.2-mile loop.

Time: 40–60 minutes.

Tread: 1.8 miles singletrack, 3.8 miles forest road, 0.6 mile pavement.

Aerobic level: Moderate.

Technical difficulty: 3 on singletrack.

Hazards: Originally designed as a pedestrian trail, the nature trail has many switchbacks, most of which are tight and narrow and need to be walked. This is a slow-speed trail for bikes, and utmost courtesy must be exercised.

Highlights: The first 1.5 miles are part of a designated scenic nature and mining history trail created by the BLM (the Mineral Ridge Trail), complete with a detailed guide and educational program. The descent is a mostly shaded,

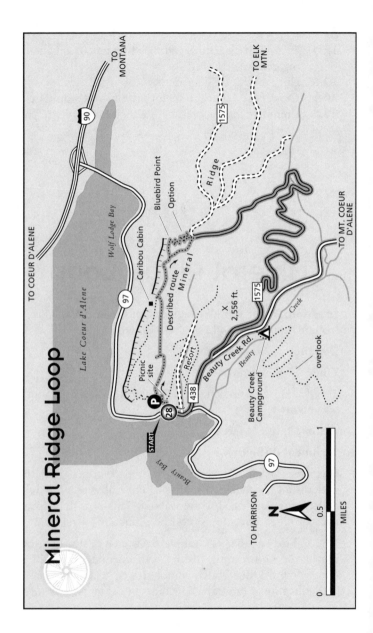

Mineral Ridge Loop

TO COEUR D'ALENE

TO MONTANA

90

Lake Coeur d'Alene

Wolf Lodge Bay

97

Caribou Cabin

Bluebird Point
Option

Ridge

1575

TO ELK MTN.

Picnic site

Described route

Mineral

Resort

X 2,556 ft.

1575

TO MT. COEUR D'ALENE

P

Beauty Creek Rd.

Beauty Creek

Beauty Creek Campground

overlook

START

Beauty Bay

28

438

97

TO HARRISON

N

0   0.5   1

MILES

nontechnical national forest road (Forest Road 1575) with a few rough spots toward the bottom. There's also an option to follow FR 1575 up to the left briefly, then take the middle track at a three-way split, which leads to the top of Elk Mountain itself, a thousand-foot vertical climb.

Land status: Bureau of Land Management, Idaho Panhandle National Forest.

Maps: Coeur d'Alene National Forest map; USGS Mount Coeur d'Alene, Idaho.

Access: From Coeur d'Alene, take Interstate 90 east about 10 miles. Turn off at exit 22 and head toward Harrison on Idaho Highway 97. Go 2 miles and turn left off ID 97 to the Mineral Ridge trailhead and picnic site. There you'll find ample parking for more than two dozen cars, potties, and drinking water. The ride starts and ends at the trailhead sign just above the parking lot.

The Ride

0.0 From the trailhead sign at the Mineral Ridge trailhead/parking lot, walk up the first 20 yards of the trail; rail tie steps with wood rail fencing frame this

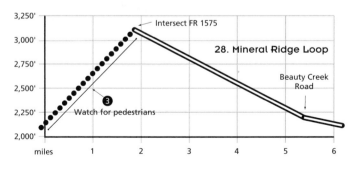

first section of trail. Climb moderate grade in a thinned canopy of pine and fir. Watch for pedestrians the first half mile, especially.

0.1 First switchback.

0.2 Switchback right. A short bit farther, stay right as the trail splits. It's a one-way loop to the right, with the return coming in here from the left.

0.3–0.8 Switchbacks with grade easing at 0.6 and getting steeper at 0.8.

0.9 Prospect Spur Trail goes left; stay right to continue route, climbing increasing grade.

1.2+ Get run at steep switchback left.

1.3 Go right at T intersection as you reach a saddle on Mineral Ridge; glide and then rise gently. This is where you leave the nature/history loop (Mineral Ridge Trail). Follow the Wilson Trail up a smooth singletrack. Sign reads: ELK MTN. RD. 1 MILE. (It's FR 1575.) There's also a drinking fountain at this T. The Caribou Cabin picnic shelter is just up to the left about 100 feet. Elevation 2,700 feet.

1.5- Go right at fork. The Elk Mountain Trail heads steeply up Mineral Ridge to the right here. Most will have to push this section (4). Option: Go left here, which will lead you through a fun and technical singletrack to Bluebird Point in about 0.2 mile; this is a great vista over Wolf Lodge Bay. Then follow the thin, steep, and somewhat overgrown singletrack through a series of switchbacks to FR 1575, about 100 feet north of where you meet this forest road on the main route.

1.8- Climb to summit of this ride (3,170 feet) and go right at FR 1575. Descend slightly from a hairpin turn. It's mostly good cruising from this point on with occasional ruts, rubble, and soft spots.

1.9 Vista of Beauty Bay to right (west).

3.3 FR 1575C goes sharp left here. Stay to main track.

3.9–4.7 Surface is rocky (2+).

5.2 Road cuts through a rock shoulder.

5.3 Pass over cattle guard.

5.5 Rocky and soft! (2+)

5.6 Go right at paved Beauty Creek Road (FR 438). Watch for traffic, and beware the narrow shoulder here. Grade flattens as you follow the lush meadows of Beauty Creek.

5.9 Cattle guard.

6.0- Go right at ID 97, which winds along the edge of Beauty Bay. Watch for traffic.

6.1 Pass by resort on your right.

6.2 Complete loop at Mineral Ridge trailhead, where you started.

Beauty Creek– Caribou Ridge

Location: About 10 miles southeast of Coeur d'Alene, between Beauty Bay and Mount Coeur d'Alene.

Distance: 13.4-mile loop.

Time: 1 hour and 45 minutes–3 hours.

Tread: 4.5 miles singletrack, 2.6 miles doubletrack/dirt road, 6.3 miles paved.

Aerobic level: Strenuous.

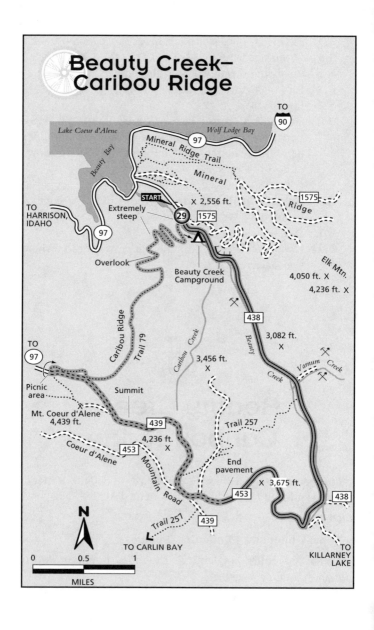

Technical difficulty: 4+ (singletrack).

Hazards: The last 2 miles of this ride are expert difficulty! Below the Caribou Ridge overlook (about mile 11.4) there exists exposed and highly hazardous trail; it's narrow, obscured by berry bushes, and not recommended for children, the timid, or even intermediate bikers. Most will want to walk the entire section between 11.5 and 13.2 miles. Also, watch for log trucks on Beauty Creek Road (Forest Road 438).

Highlights: The first 3 miles of the Caribou Ridge Trail—which starts at mile 8.6—are some of the sweetest singletrack you'll find in the entire region. The trail is also a designated National Recreation Trail. Views from the Mount Coeur d'Alene picnic site and from the Caribou Ridge overlook are impressive. Most of the climb included in this ride is at a benign gradient, following Beauty Creek itself, or contours a shady forest road.

Land status: Coeur d'Alene National Forest.

Maps: Coeur d'Alene National Forest map; USGS Mount Coeur d'Alene, Idaho.

Access: From Coeur d'Alene, take Interstate 90 east about 10 miles. Turn off at exit 22 and head toward Harrison on Idaho Highway 97. Go a little over 2 miles and turn left off

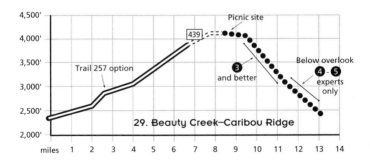

ID 97 and onto FR 438 (Beauty Creek Road), which is paved. Go 0.6 mile up FR 438 and right into the Beauty Creek Campground, and then right again to the Caribou Ridge trailhead. The ride begins and ends here. There's ample parking for more than two dozen cars.

The Ride

0.0 From the Caribou Ridge trailhead at the northwest end of Beauty Creek Campground, pedal out of the trailhead parking loop to FR 438, which is paved for the next 6 miles. Go right (south) and up FR 438, climbing gently. Elevation 2,310 feet.

0.6 Wind around rock buttress as grade increases.

0.8 Road crosses small creek, joining Beauty Creek, which you're following.

1.6 Pass cedar grove to your right.

2.0 Come out of trees into opening. Elevation 2,600 feet.

2.4 Grade steepens.

2.6 Grade levels at 2,780 feet.

2.7 Trail 257 (Carlin–Beauty Creek Trail) goes off right here. It's a singletrack option to staying on this paved route for the next 4 miles; it's much steeper and connects with the ascent route at mile 6.6-.

3.9- Stay to paved road as FR 438 splits off to the left sharply and turns to gravel. You're now on FR 453. Elevation 3,090 feet.

6.1 A great vista to the right, looking north.

6.3+ Bear right as pavement ends and road splits. Left is FR 439; follow FR 453 to right briefly, which is mostly smooth dirt.

6.4 Go right at another split; this is FR 439 now, which skirts the north side of Mount Coeur d'Alene, rising gently. Elevation 3,880 feet.

6.6- Trail 257 comes in from the right (northeast) at 3,900 feet.

7.0 Grade increases as you enter a fir-hemlock canopy.

8.0 Go right at fork to picnic site (following sign). Summit of ride is at 4,320 feet.

8.1 Cruise as you descend slightly.

8.6 Trail 79 (Caribou Ridge Trail) intersects FR 439 here at the Mount Coeur d'Alene picnic site. You'll head down to the right on singletrack, but for mileage accuracy, first go about 50 yards to the viewpoint and picnic site. It has a beautiful cedar grove, tables, and potties. Backtrack 50 yards and then head down Trail 79, a smooth singletrack in lush forest. There's a sign warning of the hazards below the overlook. The next 3 miles are mostly 3 difficulty, fun but hazardous! Experts only beyond this point! So get ready for what's to come. Elevation 4,300 feet.

8.8–8.9- Treewells (big holes left where trees have fallen) (4-).

9.0 Trail goes sidehill. Elevation 4,130 feet.

9.5 Enter meadow area, then tight and rocky turns (4).

9.6 S turns.

9.9+ Bottom out and rise slightly.

10.1 Narrow switchbacks, tight turns, big treewell (3+).

10.6- Steep downhill curves and lush growth (4).

10.7- Switchback.

10.8+ Trail widens briefly.

10.9 Rollers!

11.4 Approach overlook. Caution! Trail exposed next 2 miles. Elevation 3,100 feet.

11.6 Carry around and down rock steps, then switchback right. The next 1.6 miles of trail are narrow, exposed, and rocky. Most will want to walk their bikes this section. The worst obstacles are narrow, rocky corners, and deep treewells—4–5+!

13.2 Trail opens up as you enter cedars. Switchback around fence and cross wood bridge (3-). Elevation 2,450 feet.

13.4 Complete loop at starting point.

Silver Mountain Nature Trail

Location: Kellogg, Idaho, a half hour east of Coeur d'Alene on Interstate 90.

Distance: 2.8-mile figure-eight loop.

Time: 20–30 minutes.

Tread: 0.6 mile forest road/doubletrack, 2.2 miles singletrack.

Aerobic level: Easy.

Technical difficulty: 3.

Hazards: Tight turns over scree and sticks, and around hikers. Since a little problem arose with an adjacent large private landowner, most of the beginner to intermediate

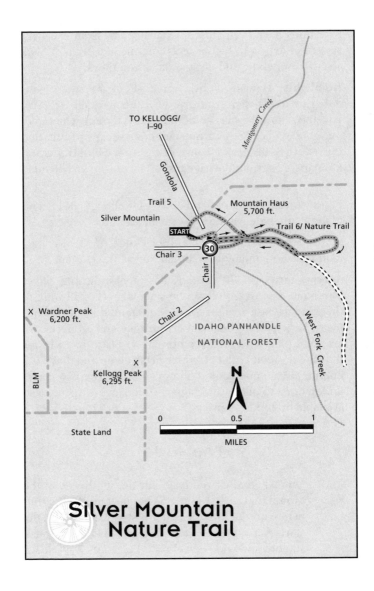

Silver Mountain
Nature Trail

bike trails have been closed; what remains is an excellent system of expert to higher level intermediate trails. Check ahead for opening and closing dates and times.

Highlights: Tight turns over scree, ski area views, a gondola ride to get there, and two chairlifts available to carry you and your bike over some very steep terrain. The top of the gondola accesses an outstanding system of trails that lead south to the St. Joe Range or east to the Bitterroots and Montana. Check out the Lake Elsie Trail, too, for an extended ride.

Land status: Ski area land (city of Kellogg), BLM, and Idaho Panhandle National Forest all around.

Maps: Silver Mountain Bike Trail Guide; USGS Kellogg, Idaho; Idaho Panhandle National Forest Travel Map.

Access: Turn off I–90 at the Kellogg exit indicating Silver Mountain Ski Area. Follow the signs about a half mile to the gondola/base area for Silver Mountain; there are a couple of large parking lots. Take your bike and all necessary gear and food with you; the normal way is to pay $10 for the all-day summer ticket, which gets you up and down the mountain via gondola and allows access to the two chairs on top open to hikers and bikers. (Food and drink are also available on top for a price.)

The Ride

0.0 Unload gondola and head out the south side of the Mountain Haus. About 100 feet beyond is a big trail map with the top of Chair 1 just beyond; this is the start and finish of your ride. Go left (east) on a smooth and wide gravel trail. Elevation 5,700 feet.

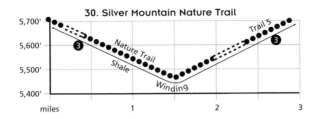

30. Silver Mountain Nature Trail

0.1 Go left and descend somewhat around the Amphitheater (there's music happening here in the summer). Track turns to rocky dirt road. Look for signs to the Nature Trail.

0.2 Go right on road, following signs to Trail 6, the Nature Trail. Just a bit farther, go left onto a rocky singletrack as it enters the trees, marked by a sign: NATURE TRAIL.

0.3 It gets rockier and bumpier real quick (2+); slow, but fun.

0.5 Go through shale S turns (3).

0.6 Catch the vista as you traverse sidehill across a scree slope (3-).

0.7 Scree surface goes to 3+.

1.2 Drop down and wind through narrow switchbacks, 3- now.

1.3 Climb a bit, rolling and rocky (3-).

1.5 Surface eases a little as you climb gently, S curves.

1.6 Bottom out and begin to climb. Elevation 5,450 feet.

1.9 Vista southwest and to Wardner Peak as scree goes 3.

2.0+ Merge right with rocky forest road, leaving single-track. Climb slightly, going north.

2.3 Pass Trail 6 loop point.

2.4- Go right onto a smooth gravel singletrack, Trail 5, as it heads into the trees, level.

- **2.5** Trail gets rocky as you pass under the gondola.
- **2.6** Switchback left, and then pass under the gondola again.
- **2.7** Bear right and uphill as you cross the ski service road between the Amphitheater and the Mountain Haus.
- **2.8** Complete loop, and maybe check out one of the more advanced rides.

Hiawatha Rail Trail

Location: On the Idaho-Montana line and south of Interstate 90 in the Bitterroots.

Distance: 15 miles out and back.

Time: 2 hours.

Tread: All-gravel-surface rail bed converted to bike and pedestrian travel.

Aerobic level: Easy to moderate.

Technical difficulty: 1.

Hazards: The Taft Tunnel at 1.8 miles in length has an ambient year-round temperature of 33 degrees F; it's also pitch-black and requires a good light. A halogen bulb will throw much more light than a standard bulb. Passing cyclists in opposite directions require extra attention in this long tunnel and in the other shorter ones, too (I had a

Hiawatha Rail Trail

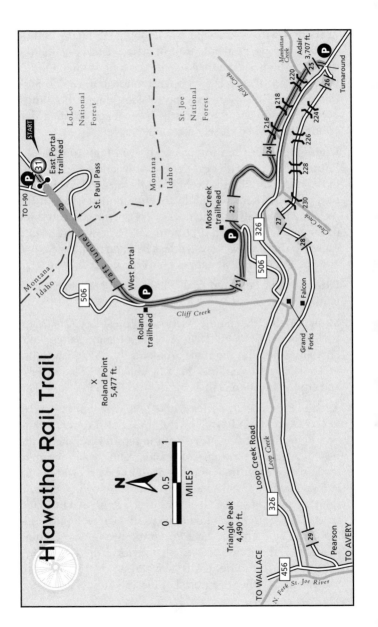

near miss with a kid who was looking up at the ceiling while zooming past our group). Also, watch out for the drainage ditches on either side of the long tunnel. One 2-mile section of trail is also open to auto traffic. The high trestles, some over 200 feet, have 4-foot-plus-high railings. Some exposure near the trestle approaches requires that young children be closely escorted.

Highlights: With ten tunnels and seven high trestles, the Route of the Hiawatha on the old Milwaukee Road is one of the premier rail trails in the United States today. The portion given here in this guide covers the upper half of the reclaimed rail trail and includes six of the tunnels and three of the trestles. The trail drops only 300 feet in more than 7 miles, so the grade is very gentle. The Bitterroot, the St. Joe, and the Coeur d'Alene ranges converge here.

Land status: Lolo and Idaho Panhandle National Forest land.

Maps: Idaho Panhandle National Forest Visitors Map; USGS topos: St. Paul Pass, Montana-Idaho, Saltese and Shefoot Mountain, Montana; Lookout Pass Ski Area Route of the Hiawatha Rail Trail map (available at Lookout Pass and from the trail marshals on the trail).

Access: From Coeur d'Alene, take I–90 east about 60 miles to exit O, Lookout Pass Ski Area, if you need to rent a bike or a light or to arrange for a shuttle return ride; this is the headquarters of the trail concession. Otherwise, if you're ready to roll, continue another 5 miles east into Montana and take exit 5. From there, go left at T, following signs to Route of the Hiawatha. Go a little over a tenth of a mile and take a right onto Forest Road 506 (Rainy Creek Road). Follow another 2 miles to East Portal trailhead. As you come in sight of the trailhead, bear left at fork; there's parking here. Going to the right will take you up over the Roland Summit and to the west portal of the Taft Tunnel (for those who don't want to travel the long tunnel but still want access to the rail trail). The ride starts and ends at the road separating the trail from the parking lot.

The Ride

0.0   From the East Portal trailhead, pedal southwest (through the wood arch and toward the Taft Tunnel, elevation 4,147 feet). A trail marshal may be here to collect fees and provide information.

0.2   Enter the Taft Tunnel. Make sure to have your lights on. If you're in a group, stay together and your shared light will make it easier for everyone to see.

2.0- Come out of the tunnel at the West Portal. A 30-foot waterfall drops down just to the north side.

2.2   FR 506 joins with the rail trail here at Roland trail-head from the west. Caution! For the next 2 miles, autos share the trail until Moss Creek trailhead. The trail until that point is part of FR 506.

2.3   Arrive at the Roland trailhead. Auto parking and potties are here, too.

2.7   Pass a large slate rock outcropping.

2.9   Pass another large rock outcropping.

3.5   Enter Tunnel 21; it's almost 800 feet long, and it's curved.

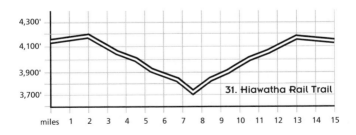

31. Hiawatha Rail Trail

4.2+ Come to the Moss Creek trailhead. Leave motorized access at this point as FR 506 veers off right and down.

4.5 Enter Tunnel 22, which is over 1,500 feet long. The surface in this tunnel is a bit slimy; it feels like wet clay, so exercise caution here.

5.1 Pass another large rock face.

5.3 As you approach Tunnel 23, the trail detours around it. This one was built on a fault line and is not considered safe now.

5.6 Enter Tunnel 24.

5.7 Cross the Small Creek Trestle (#216). A six-strand steel cable railing protects travelers.

6.0 Cross the Barnes Creek Trestle (#218).

6.2 A historical marker points to a grave marked with a cross here. This death was connected with a 1910 fire. Read the marker for the story. The trail surface at this point is larger, unconsolidated gravel and so yields a bumpier ride.

6.6- Cross the Kelly Creek Trestle (#220). This is the highest trestle on the route (230 feet) and so deserves the seven-strand railing.

7.5 Come to the old rail stop at Adair (elevation 3,707 feet). This is a lush spot with markers, a creek, and Tunnel 25 just ahead, which will be your turn-around point. This is a great spot for lunch, and it's also about halfway on the reclaimed rail trail. Proceed through the curved tunnel, turn around, and go back the way you came.

To see the full Hiawatha route, you'd have to pedal to Pearson, which would take you through another four tunnels and over another four trestles. The full route, from East Portal to Pearson and back, is about 30 miles. Also consider that connections to forest roads and trails from East

Portal and Pearson will loop you back to Wallace or lead you into three mountain ranges that converge here. Take your pick of old mines, high lakes, and historic ghost towns. Acquaint yourself with the hazards of this and other mining districts. Ask locals and staff at Lookout Pass and on the trail. This trail was buffed by hundreds of people, working thousands of hours to make it accessible to tourists and even wheelchairs. Outside of this corridor, things can get rugged.

Spirit Lake– Larch Mountain

Location: North side of Spirit Lake, Idaho; 40 minutes northeast of Spokane.

Distance: 7.1-mile loop.

Time: 40–60 minutes.

Tread: 3.7 miles pavement, 2.8 miles forest road/double-track, 0.6 mile singletrack.

Aerobic level: Easy to moderate.

Technical difficulty: 2+ with a short downhill of 4.

Hazards: Autos on Spirit Lake Road; log trucks on M41; one-half mile steep downhill singletrack.

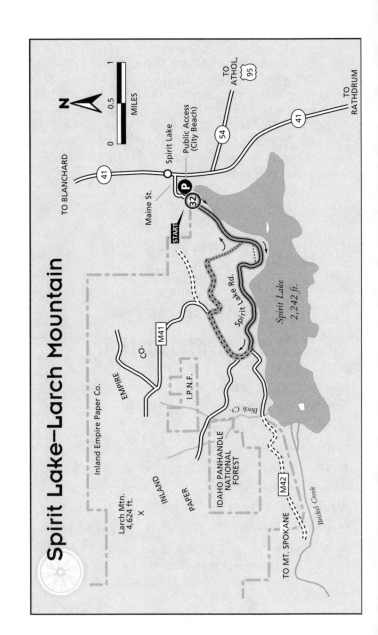

Spirit Lake–Larch Mountain

Highlights: Great views of Spirit Lake, not to mention the funky little town itself; a short but screaming downhill section just to shake you out of complacency.

Land status: County road, Inland Empire Paper Co. land (nonmotorized open to public).

Maps: USGS Spirit Lake West, Spirit Lake East; Idaho Panhandle National Forest Travel Map (Coeur d'Alene district).

Access: Thirty miles northeast of Spokane is Spirit Lake, Idaho. Idaho Highway 41 is the main thoroughfare going north-south. Go west off ID 41 at Maine (local humor) Street; there'll also be a sign: Spirit Lake Public Access (important because the lake access is almost entirely private). Following Maine Street leads you through the old (and genuine) western town of Spirit Lake. Keep to Maine as it leads you out of the commercial district down through a series of curves. In less than a half mile, pull in left to the Spirit Lake Public Access (city beach and boat launch). Here you'll find ample parking, potties, an inn across the street, even shade. The ride starts and ends in the middle of the parking area.

The Ride

0.0 Pedal out of the parking area and go left (west) on the Spirit Lake Road (paved). Elevation 2,500 feet.

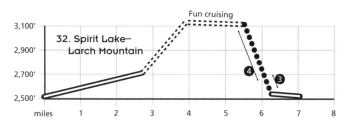

0.1 Pass over earth bridge that crosses the northern arm of the lake.

0.2 Climb moderate hill through rock cuts.

0.3 Crest and swoop into conifers and fun curves. Watch for traffic all along this north road; there's not a lot of shoulder. The next 2.4 miles are winding, climbing, dropping, and swooping, and almost all of this stretch is in the shade on smooth pavement.

2.7 Go up a steep hill right, off the pavement, and through a barrier gate. A sign marks this rocky dirt/gravel logging road as M41. The name is Inland Empire Paper's: This is their land and nomenclature for this main artery that connects through to Blanchard, to the north side of Larch Mountain. Elevation 2,700 feet.

2.9 Switchback up through rock cut, moderately steep.

3.0 Follow main road through switchback right as another log road cuts left.

3.2 Wind and climb steep hill.

3.9 Go right off M41 and onto a level and mostly smooth doubletrack. Elevation 3,150 feet. Glide, crank, and zoom this fun section.

4.6 Dip through drainage and climb out.

5.2 Climb moderate hill with softer sand (3-). Elevation 3,120 feet.

5.5 Plunge right, down a steep dirt singletrack (ATV track) that follows the fall line. Caution! You may want to walk this section; sticks and chunks contribute to the excitement here (4).

5.9+ Bear left as a wide singletrack/ATV trail intersects your path. Wind around through a level meadow.

6.0 Stay right on main ATV trail where a doubletrack heads left into trees.

6.1 Wind around, up, and through a mound of stumps and earth (3+). Go left at pavement; this is the north-side road you came in on. Elevation 2,620 feet.

6.3 Climb gentle to moderate grade.

6.8 Crest and glide as trees give way to open shoreline.

7.1 Complete loop back at parking area near the beach.

Spirit Lake–
Brickel Creek

Location: From Spirit Lake, Idaho, to Mount Spokane, Washington, via Brickel Creek.

Distance: 30.8 miles, out and back.

Time: 2.5 to 4 hours.

Tread: 8 miles pavement, 22.8 miles forest road/double-track.

Aerobic level: Strenuous.

Technical difficulty: 3–4 off pavement.

Hazards: Autos on Spirit Lake Road; numerous stream crossings, big ruts, big rocks, soft spots, and a low canopy in places. Bring water, even if you can beg it at the condos or the inn at the top of this ride.

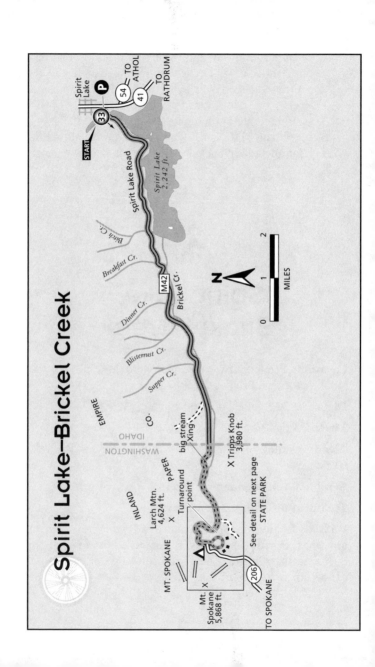

Spirit Lake–Brickel Creek

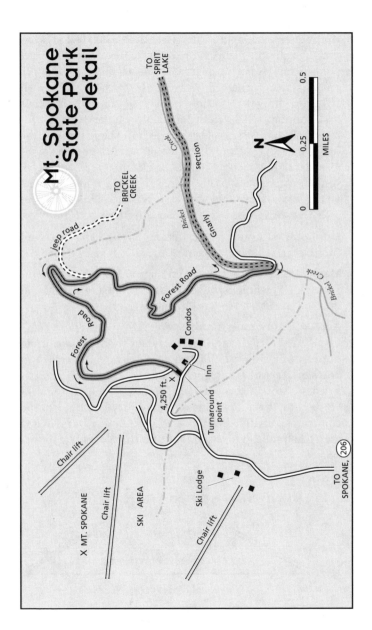

Highlights: At 30+ miles and more than 2,000 feet of accumulative climbing, this is the biggest ride of the book, yet not one mile is boring or porcine. From smooth but curvy cruising to a sustained yet friendly grade with enough obstacles thrown in to hold your attention, this out-and-back shows you a different personality on the descent. Facing north and east, it offers almost full shade most of the route; it stays cool and protected on even the hottest summer days. Following Brickel Creek on an old rail bed, you're treated to waterfalls, pools, and hidden little pockets of life while ascending at a civilized rate. Wildlife, from owls to cougars, are here, so keep your bear bells on.

Land status: County road, Inland Empire Paper Co. land (nonmotorized open to public).

Maps: USGS Spirit Lake West, Spirit Lake East, Mount Spokane, Washington/Idaho; Idaho Panhandle National Forest Travel Map (Coeur d'Alene district).

Access: Thirty miles northeast of Spokane is Spirit Lake, Idaho. Idaho Highway 41 is the main thoroughfare going north-south. Go west off ID 41 at Maine Street; there'll also be a sign: SPIRIT LAKE PUBLIC ACCESS. Follow Maine Street as it leads through the old (and genuine) western town of Spirit Lake. Keep to Maine and it will lead you out of the commercial district down through a series of curves. In less than a half mile, pull in left to the Spirit Lake Public Access

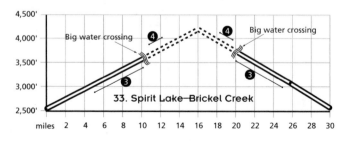

(city beach and boat launch). Here you'll find ample parking, potties, an inn across the street, even shade. The ride starts and ends in the middle of the parking area.

The Ride

0.0 Pedal out of the parking area and go left (west) on Spirit Lake Road (paved). Elevation 2,500 feet.

0.1 Pass over earth bridge that crosses northern arm of lake.

0.2 Climb moderate hill through rock cuts.

0.3 Crest and swoop into conifers and fun curves. Watch for traffic all along this north road; there's not a lot of shoulder. The next 3.7 miles wind, climb, drop, and swoop over shady pavement. Beware of everything from log trucks to ATVs.

4.0+ Continue on past the end of the pavement; surface turns to gravel as grade descends moderately. This is now Inland Empire Paper Company land, road M42. Technical difficulty 2+. The next 6 miles roll and wind, gaining elevation gradually.

9.0 Bear left at fork, staying with Brickel Creek.

10.3 Road ends and splits into two singletracks. Take the left one, which leads to Brickel Creek. Cross creek (carry bike) over big round rocks; water can be 1 to 2 feet deep. Continue up and across the other side to doubletrack again; climb big rocks, short steep grade (4+), which—along with the surface—mellows after a short time to big ruts under a dense canopy of cedar (3+).

10.9 Pass a 50-foot-high rock to your left.

11.1 Climb (4-).

11.3 Crest, then cross Brickel Creek again over big round rock (4+). Elevation 3,300 feet.

11.4 Climb gently through grassy meadow and big ruts.

11.6 Cross small stream and seep (4).

11.7 Cross Brickel Creek (4+).

12.1 Pick a line as you climb moderately; water flowing down ruts will detour most around the center of the trail (4).

12.2 Doubletrack goes off right; stay to main trail.

12.7 Bear right as the trail meets a wider, sandy forest road. Surface and grade actually ease from this point on, but watch for sticks, soft spots, and ruts (3-).

13.3 Cross creek.

13.9 Doubletrack goes right; stay left.

14.2 Switchback left, then go around cattle guard.

15.0- Cross small creek.

15.3 Arrive at pavement (surprise!) by a basketball hoop and backboard. You're at a big parking lot just above the Snowblaze Condos at the Mount Spokane ski area. A little outdoor chapel stands just left of an inn; if you're lucky, you can get a meal and something to drink. This is the top and turnaround point for this ride; for mileage sake, I allow two-tenths of a mile to tool around and check things out before heading back down. Lots of options from here, though: Another 1,500 vertical feet of pedaling up right on the pavement will lead to the Vista House (top of Mount Spokane), which is visible, along with chairlifts to the north. You can even pedal the 25 miles back to Spokane if you're not burdened by a car at Spirit Lake. Elevation 4,250 feet.

18.2 Go left and down at split, the way you came. It turns to 3 quickly.

20.5 Last crossing of Brickel Creek; doubletrack turns to gravel road just beyond.

26.7 Gravel goes to pavement here. Cruise and wind the last 4 miles.

30.8 Complete loop back at parking lot by beach. Now consider the possibilities of the side routes passed by, between here and Mount Spokane, for a return visit.

Farragut State Park: Shoreline Trail

Location: Farragut State Park, 4 miles east of U.S. Highway 95 between Coeur d'Alene and Sandpoint, Idaho.

Distance: 5.8-mile loop.

Time: 30–50 minutes.

Tread: 0.1 mile pavement, 5.7 miles singletrack.

Aerobic level: Easy.

Technical difficulty: 3+.

Hazards: Watch for hikers, joggers, and kids on trails; this can be a congested area, especially on weekends and holidays. Roots, rocks, and occasional ruts can be found, along with some steep and narrow sections of trail; none of these are sustained, however.

Highlights: This is some of the most consistent and fun singletrack to be found anywhere in the region, and the trail is just a sample of what else is to be found in this park. Farragut is also an old World War II naval base, and to this

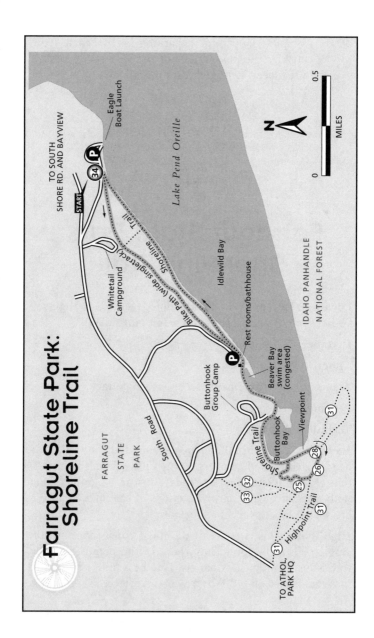

Farragut State Park: Shoreline Trail

TO SOUTH SHORE RD. AND BAYVIEW

START

Eagle Boat Launch

Lake Pend Oreille

Whitetail Campground

Bike Path (wide singletrack)

Shoreline Trail

Idlewild Bay

Rest rooms/bathhouse

Buttonhook Group Camp

Beaver Bay swim area (congested)

Viewpoint

FARRAGUT STATE PARK

South Road

Shoreline Trail

Buttonhook Bay

Highpoint Trail

25

26

28

31

31

32

33

31

34

TO ATHOL, PARK HQ

IDAHO PANHANDLE NATIONAL FOREST

N

MILES

0   0.5

day, nearby Bayview harbors a naval research facility. There are ample opportunities for exploring and learning about the history of this unique area. Swimming and overnight camping are other possibilities.

Land status: Farragut State Park land.

Maps: Farragut State Park map; USGS Bayview, Idaho.

Access: From Athol, Idaho, between Coeur d'Alene and Sandpoint on U.S. Highway 95, go east on Idaho Highway 54 a little over 4 miles. Just past the first park entrance booth, pull in right at the park headquarters. This is a visitor center with information, maps, and rest room facilities. There's a $3.00 fee per vehicle for day use. From here, proceed on South Road (the first right after the park headquarters) about 2 miles to a multipictograph park sign indicating a boat ramp (among other things) to the right and down a hill. Take this right; it leads to the Eagle Boat Launch. Your ride starts and ends in the boat launch parking lot.

The Ride

0.0 Start mileage from the DO NOT ENTER signs where the boat launch road loops back to the main parking area. Pedal west to just where you entered the parking area from the spur off South Road. Go through

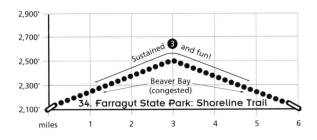

175

stiles that lead you onto a wide bike path; the surface starts as old asphalt but quickly deteriorates to dirt.

0.1   Climb a gentle grade.

0.4   Go left at fork and trail sign, staying to this bike path. Right leads to South Road. Descend moderate grade.

1.0   Descend a short, steep, and rocky grade (2).

1.1   Go left off main bike path, then immediately right onto Shoreline Trail, which is narrower and has more obstacles (2+). This is just before you come to the Beaver Bay parking lot. The trail now skirts along between the parking lot and the lakeshore.

1.3   Arrive at Beaver Bay swim area. Go right and up some wide gravel steps and then left before the swim area rest rooms. This will allow you to continue on the Shoreline Trail, which resumes dirt as it descends down to the water on the north side of the bay. Caution! This is a highly congested area, so it's best to walk your bike until the crowds thin out.

1.5   Climb away from swim area; turns to 3+ as obstacles increase. Then, at split, stay left to main trail.

1.7   Stay left to main trail at fork as trail descends briefly; rest rooms are to right.

1.8   At Buttonhook Bay, bear right at boat docks where you briefly join gravel road. Then go left onto singletrack as trail skirts north shore of bay. Rollers (3) are fun in here.

2.2   Climb through curves and trail bars (3+) as you enter a full canopy of growth.

2.3   Negotiate a 3+ slide area, rocky.

2.4- Reach an opening with Trail 31 marker. This is a nice little vista of the lake, complete with bench and bubbling brook. Go right up gentle grade, following rivulet.

2.6 Pass Highpoint Trail to your left. Trail 27 comes in from the right (you'll be coming back this way). Continue through the junction straight ahead.

2.7 Turn right onto Trail 28, just before wire fence and park boundary. This is a great, winding section of trail: rocks, tight trees, fun (3)!

3.0- Come to a place of thinner trees. Trail 26 goes left, but stay right, and in another 50 feet, stay right again where Trail 25 goes left. Now descend through banked, air-prone curves in thick woods! Elevation 2,500 feet.

3.3- Go right at split in wooded saddle.

3.3+ Loop back to Shoreline Trail, heading left and the way you came. Highpoint Trail is straight ahead. Descend technical, fun section.

4.1 At the northeast end of Buttonhook Bay go left.

4.5 At Beaver Bay rest rooms, go left just past them and along a gravel trail that leads to the parking area (paved), not down the way you came. Then pedal through the parking lot to the east end. Of course, you're watching that lady with the big hair in the big sedan who has you in her rearview mirror crosshair.

4.6 Go off pavement right onto singletrack dirt, Shoreline Trail, shady and mostly 3 minimum for the remainder of the ride. For the next mile, you dance along the water.

4.8–5.0 Boulders, roots, sand, marbles—the stuff of heaven (3+)!

5.2 Stay right at fork.

5.3–5.6 Rugged, rolling (4-).

5.6 Go left and up steep dirt trail, leaving Shoreline Trail. A couple of warning stakes are here. The trail actually continues through to the boat ramp, but it's badly washed and now closed.

5.6+ Bear right back onto the wide bike trail that you first started on. Cruise to complete loop at 5.8 miles.

Farragut State Park: North Perimeter

Location: Farragut State Park, 4 miles east of U.S. Highway 95 between Coeur d'Alene and Sandpoint, Idaho.

Distance: 10.5-mile loop.

Time: 60–90 minutes.

Tread: 3.2 miles pavement, 4.3 miles forest road/double-track, 3 miles singletrack.

Aerobic level: Moderate.

Technical difficulty: 3- in the dirt.

Hazards: Watch for hikers, bikers, horses, and kids; can be congested, especially on weekends and holidays. Some punji stakes, especially on the outer roads.

Highlights: This ride is an introduction to an area of the park most folks never see; if you go off onto any of the splits, you'll find surprises and bits of Idaho history. Farragut is also an old (World War II–era) naval base, and to this day, nearby Bayview harbors a naval research facility; there are ample opportunities for exploring and learning

Farragut State Park: North Perimeter

Bayview Road/Perimeter Road

Scenic Bay

Bayview

Water tower Old pavement

South Road

Locust Grove Picnic Area

Snowberry Campground

Whitetail Campground

Eagle boat launch

Lake Pend Oreille

Shoreline Trail

Bike path

35

Beaver Bay swim area

START

Amphitheater

Pt. 3

Pt. 2

FARRAGUT

STATE

Road

North

Pt. 5

Pt. 15

Pt. 14

Shooting range

TO CAREYWOOD

Water tower

Pt. 11

Boy Scout Friendship Poles

PARK

South Road

54

Park HQ/ Visitor Center

Thimbleberry Group Area

95

TO ATHOL

N

MILES

0   0.5   1

about the history of this unique area. Swimming and overnight camping are available, too.

Land status: Farragut State Park land.

Maps: Farragut State Park map; USGS Bayview, Idaho.

Access: From Athol, Idaho, between Coeur d'Alene and Sandpoint on US 95, go east on Idaho Highway 54 a little over 4 miles. Just past the first park entrance booth, pull in right at the park headquarters. This is a visitor center with information, maps, and rest room facilities. There's a $3.00 fee per vehicle for day use. From here, proceed on South Road east (bear right coming out of the park headquarters) 1.9 miles to the Beaver Bay swim area; go right and down a hill. The ride starts and ends in the Beaver Bay swim area parking lot, by the rest rooms and showers.

The Ride

0.0 Pedal east through the paved parking lot. This is probably the most dangerous part of the ride!

0.1 Head off the pavement, through bollards, and onto a wide bike path (old pavement, deteriorating to dirt). This is just left and slightly uphill from the Shoreline Trail; both trails are covered by a full canopy.

0.2 Climb short, steep slope (3-).

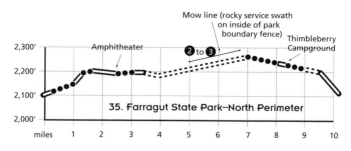

0.9 Go left off bike path 100 feet, then right onto pavement; this is Whitetail Campground.

1.0 Climb moderate grade.

1.1 Go through the campground gate, and then go right (east) on South Road (also paved). Signs here indicate the Snowberry Campground left and Eagle Boat Launch right.

1.2+ Take the second singletrack left into the woods/meadows and off South Road. Note: A number of trails interconnect here (for the next quarter mile). If you get off/onto another trail, no problem! You're veering around north and east of Snowberry Campground, trying to get to the old military loop road (paved, but partly closed to autos now) that circles Locust Grove Picnic Area. Any number of these trails will get you to the upper road; you can even go right through the campground, if you like.

1.3 At three-way split, go right along north rim of gully.

1.4+ Just before mile 1.4, take Y to the right (3-); fun dips! Hug perimeter of Snowberry Campground. Go right at another Y and up through meadow.

1.6+ Just before mile 1.6, go up left at a T (3-). Then it's a short, steep ride up. Go right on pavement; this is the old base road noted earlier. Locust Grove Picnic Area is just north on the hill above you. Cruise.

2.1 Water tower to your left.

2.8- Go around steel gate and then left, crossing Idaho Highway 54. Watch for traffic!

2.9 Go right and off ID 54 just past a large state historical marker: BAYVIEW LIMEKILNS; check it out and look for remnants, if you're interested. Pass through boulders and right where two singletracks diverge. The left track will plunge you down through the bottom of the Amphitheater (a huge, carved-out hollow that's looking natural now), while the right one you're following skirts gently down and around the north rim of it. It's round rock and a bit bumpy. Pass a potty to your right, just past the boulders.

3.1 Climb marbles and golf balls (3). Then, note single-track dirt going right into dense woods, as you stay left to the wider trail.

3.2 Climb moderate grade on more marbles (3), and then go right on old pavement (North Road).

3.4 Go right through gate and down gravel road, descending moderately.

3.5+ At three-way fork, take middle singletrack, which may be obscured. This is Point 2 on the state park map. Trail widens to doubletrack after a bit.

3.7 Go left at Point 3 (on park map), which is a Y; right will lead you toward the town of Bayview.

3.8 Drop moderately as surface gets rough (3-).

4.6 Through clear-cut, threetrack now.

4.7 Climb hill up doubletrack; this is Point 5 on park map. Trail then gets rougher (chunks, punjies, wet spots) (3-).

5.7- Go left at park boundary cyclone fence, climb hill, up mow line.

6.0+ Go right at Point 15 where track follows fence. Surface mellows and flattens.

6.3+ Go left at Point 14, following fence.

6.8 Crest hill.

6.9+ Pass Point 11 and a singletrack to the left, keeping to fence.

7.3+ Trail turns back into singletrack as it sweeps left and away from fence line. It's into the woods for some winding fun!

7.5- Out of the woods (west water tower is briefly visible here) as the smooth, winding path tests your quickness (3-).

7.6 Cross North Road (old pavement) and continue east on more fun singletrack.

7.8 Come to smooth gravel road, climbing gently as you bear toward Bernard Peak in the distance.

7.9- Bear left at old asphalt Y, with water tower to the right.

8.0 Just before old apple tree to your left, bear right onto thin singletrack heading off through thistles. This track becomes more distinct as it turns to a smooth, sandy ribbon.

8.3+ Cross old asphalt road with connector road just right; keep to singletrack that cuts right through. Then bear left onto dirt road in front of wood rail corrals.

8.4 Go left and into woods, passing Thimbleberry Group Area rest rooms.

8.5 Pick up wide dirt singletrack that leads down and through forest. Watch for kids, bikes, and horses in here as you swoop through a fun, curving section of trail.

8.7 Cross old gravel road and continue on wider single-track now.

8.8- Pass Friendship Poles to right.

8.9 Pass another scout monument as the trail goes to doubletrack in a meadow. Then, go right at Y in gravel road.

9.0 Cross ID 54 onto sandy/gravel road. Caution!

9.1 Pass Brig Museum to your left. Surface goes paved now.

9.3 Go left at split.

9.4 Go right at split.

9.5 Go left on South Road. Caution! Watch for autos at highway speeds. Cruise.

9.8 Go right off South Road to Beaver Bay; zoom this hill only if you can brake like a car.

10.5 Complete loop back at Beaver Bay swim area parking lot.

Cape Horn– Three Sisters

Location: About midway between Coeur d'Alene and Sandpoint, Idaho; east of U.S. Highway 95, from Bayview, Idaho.

Distance: 13.7 miles out and back.

Time: 3–4 hours.

Tread: 0.4 miles pavement, 9.9 miles forest road, 3.4 miles singletrack.

Aerobic level: Strenuous.

Technical difficulty: 4 (singletrack).

Hazards: Some rutted and rocky sections on Forest Road 297; also watch for motor vehicles on this road. The singletrack is relatively gnarly; initially built as a pack trail and subsequently maintained as a dirt-bike trail, it can be steep and rugged. It is recommended for experienced riders only. Also, if you don't like to climb, this ride is not for you.

Highlights: This trail is one leg of an epic ride that follows an undulating spine between Blacktail Mountain to the

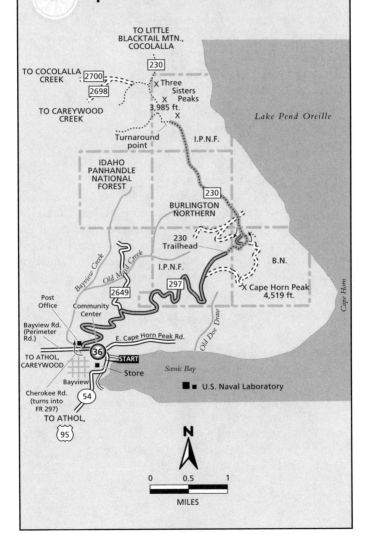

Cape Horn–Three Sisters

TO LITTLE
BLACKTAIL MTN.,
COCOLALLA

230

TO COCOLALLA
CREEK

2700
2698

TO CAREYWOOD
CREEK

X Three
Sisters
X Peaks
3,985 ft.
X

Lake Pend Oreille

Turnaround
point

I.P.N.F.

IDAHO
PANHANDLE
NATIONAL
FOREST

230

BURLINGTON
NORTHERN

230
Trailhead

B.N.

I.P.N.F.

X Cape Horn Peak
4,519 ft.

2649

297

Bayview Creek

Old Mud Creek

Post
Office

Community
Center

Old Doe Draw

Cape Horn

Bayview Rd.
(Perimeter
Rd.)

E. Cape Horn Peak Rd.

36

START

TO ATHOL,
CAREYWOOD

Store

Scenic Bay

Bayview

54

Cherokee Rd.
(turns into
FR 297)

TO ATHOL,
95

■ ■ U.S. Naval Laboratory

N

0   0.5   1

MILES

north and Cape Horn Peak to the south. The spine itself, a part of the Selkirk Mountains, towers 2,500 feet over Lake Pend Oreille (pronounced Pond aRAY), and provides numerous vistas of the lake just east and the Purcell Trench just west. This ride may be integrated with sections of the Cocolalla–Butler Creek Loop (Ride 37) and Careywood Road for a full-day, 40-mile loop.

Land status: Idaho Panhandle National Forest and Burlington Northern.

Maps: Idaho Panhandle National Forest Map; USGS Bayview and Cocolalla, Idaho.

Access: From Athol, Idaho (on US 95 between Coeur d'Alene and Sandpoint, Idaho), go east on Idaho Highway 54 about 8 miles to Bayview. In Bayview, just past the Merc (the main grocery store in town), go left on Bayview Road. About a half mile up this paved road, pull in left to the Bayview Community Center. There's ample parking at the paved/gravel lot; be sure to park back from the Children's Center, where day-care traffic is frequent. The ride starts and ends here.

The Ride

0.0	From the Bayview Community Center, go left (west) on paved Bayview Road. Elevation 2,150 feet.
0.1	Turn right onto Cherokee Road (FR 297); it's marked and just before the Bayview Post Office.
0.2	Surface turns to gravel.
0.4	Begin climbing a moderate, rocky (2) grade.
0.5	Switchback through an increasing grade.
0.8	Surface gets rough and rocky.
1.3	Grade flattens at 2,500-foot elevation.
1.5	Switchback rocky and steep.

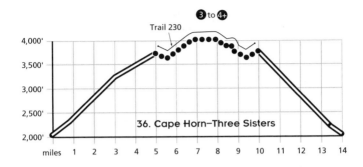

3 to 4+

Trail 230

4,000'
3,500'
3,000'
2,500'
2,000'

36. Cape Horn–Three Sisters

miles 1 2 3 4 5 6 7 8 9 10 11 12 13 14

1.8 Steep again.

1.9 Road forks. Stay on FR 297 to right as FR 2649 goes left in a saddle.

2.3 Grade mellows as road winds through posted sewer meadow area. Smells okay.

2.8 Surface gets rocky as grade goes moderate; good shade, though.

3.1 Stay to right on FR 297 as forest road splits left. Elevation 3,200 feet.

3.7 Again, stay right on FR 297 as road splits left.

4.2 A great vista opens up east as grade flattens around hairpin turn left.

4.3–4.4 Rocky!

4.6 Vista to west of the Purcell Trench and Mount Spokane. Grade drops slightly.

4.8 Take FR 230 left at fork; a Forest Service sign indicates a trail that way. This road, although overgrown, is flat and smooth.

5.0 Go left where road splits into a singletrack left and a skid trail (doubletrack) up and right. This is the trailhead for Trail 230 (Forest Service hiking sign here). The trail is smooth dirt as it drops briefly through a draw (gully). Watch out for ATVs and horses. Elevation 3,800 feet.

5.2 Cross rocky logging road, staying to singletrack. Trail now goes narrow and rocky (3+).

5.4 Begin descent down sustained steep, narrow, and rocky trail (4-). Lake is visible to east and forest road winds down around you west.

5.6 Again, cross road and resume singletrack, dropping steeply on difficult surface (4).

5.7 Bottom out and begin to climb (3).

5.8 Grade levels through brushy, narrow trail.

5.9 Drop through a couple of steep, rutted switchbacks (4).

6.0 Grade levels in draw; climb a steep 4 out; it's wider here, though.

6.1 Surface mellows and a vista opens up.

6.2 Climb 4+, rocky and narrow, then easier.

6.3 Drop through draw and climb out (3).

6.4 Climb through loose rock (4+).

6.5 Crest at 4,000 feet and a vista. Trail turns into rollers; surface improves.

6.8 You're on the South Sister now. This is the summit and your turnaround point. Elevation 4,150 feet. You can drop down another steep draw on this trail (number 230X) and get to the middle Sister within another mile, or even extend it all the way to the Blacktails and Bimetallic Ridge. For this ride, though, it's back the way you came, with one detour in 1.3 miles.

8.1 Go right and up a well-graded forest road that winds around west of the steep and rocky single-track that you came down to get here. Moderate-steep climb, but wide and easy.

8.3 Crest and glide.

8.4 Bear right at big, rocky clearing, and then go right down singletrack dirt that you came up. Swoop and roll.

8.6 Come to start of Trail 230 and sign. Bear right on doubletrack dirt flat.

8.8 Bear right and back down FR 297. Watch for kelly humps, ruts, rocks, and motors.

13.6 Go left at Bayview Road.

13.7 Complete loop at Bayview Community Center.

Cocolalla–Butler Creek Loop

Location: East of Cocolalla Lake and U.S. Highway 95, about 11 miles south of Sandpoint, Idaho.

Distance: 10.4-mile loop.

Time: 90–120 minutes.

Tread: 2.1 miles singletrack, 8.3 miles forest road.

Aerobic level: Moderate to strenuous.

Technical difficulty: Up to 4 on singletrack (mostly tight and fast downhill).

Hazards: Logging trucks and other traffic on roads. Round rock, soft spots, everyday forest debris. Motorcycles, horses, and berry pickers, sometimes all in the same spot.

Highlights: The maintenance work done on this trail in the late 1990s has helped a lot. Trail 231, which you follow on the downhill swoop, anchors the northern end of the

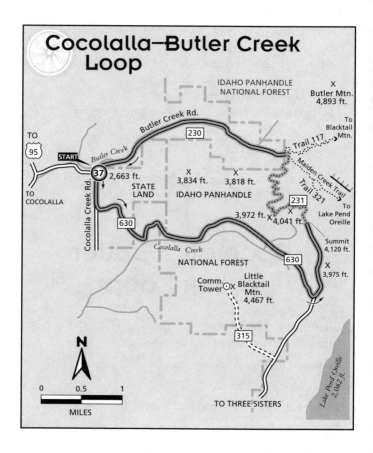

Cocolalla–Butler Creek Loop

Blacktail–Three Sisters ridgeline on the west edge of Lake Pend Oreille. You can connect to Trail 230 to the south for mixed singletrack all the way to Cape Horn Peak, Bayview, and Farragut State Park. Other tracks (marked and unmarked) can be found between Little Blacktail and Bimetallic Ridge.

Land status: Idaho Panhandle National Forest.

Maps: Idaho Panhandle National Forest Travel Map; USGS Cocolalla, Idaho.

Access: Eleven miles south of Sandpoint, Idaho, turn east off US 95 on Blacktail Road. Coming from Coeur d'Alene, it's about midway at Cocolalla Lake. Go left at the road split 0.7 mile from US 95; the surface turns to gravel. At 1.5 miles from the highway, park on state land on the east side of the junction of Butler Creek Road (Forest Road 230) and Careywood Road (county). A large fir provides shade, and there's ample room for parking. The ride starts and ends at this junction.

The Ride

0.0 Go south on Cocolalla Creek Road (gravel, county) that meets Butler Creek Road (FR 230); it's flat and dusty in the summer. Elevation 2,800 feet.

0.2 Climb a moderate-steep hill.

0.5 Go left (east) on FR 630. Climb gentle to moderate grade.

0.7 Crest at 2,950 feet and glide. Then climb moderate to gentle grade.

2.4 Stay left as gated forest road goes right.

3.6–4.0 Climb through steep, rocky sections.

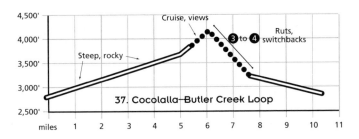

4.4 FR 630 splits into two roads, going both ways. Go left and up. There's also a hiking trail sign that indicates either direction.

4.9 Stay to right where doubletrack goes off left. Elevation 3,740 feet.

5.2 Climb out of trees, rocky (2).

5.4 Bear right where a ditch cuts across the intersection of an older logging road and this one.

5.4+ Go left onto a smooth dirt singletrack. Doubletrack goes off right. Cruise fun trail.

5.7 Reach a small crest.

5.8 Cruise easy grade. Maiden Creek Canyon walls are visible to the east. This section of trail hugs the edge of the ridgeline, offering breezes, views, and berries. Elevation 4,040 feet.

6.1+ Grade eases. Elevation 4,090 feet.

6.2 Crest at a rocky clearing and the summit. Elevation 4,120 feet. Then drop quickly into woods and tight turns (4). Get ready to strap on your rocket packs; maybe check your binders first. Switchback down a steep hillside in cedars and broken trees.

7.5 Doubletrack resumes as you bottom out in draw, the top of Maiden Creek drainage. Elevation 3,330 feet.

7.6- Bear left onto Butler Creek Road (FR 230) after passing Trail 321 (down Maiden Creek) on your right. Trail 117 (a steep set of switchbacks to the top of Blacktail Mountain) also goes right at the end of a small loop/turnaround. Just bear left at this junction and you'll find yourself heading northwest on the main forest road. Detours from this lush pocket are possible from here; there's even an old cemetery just north. It's mostly mid- to high-speed cruising from here, descending Butler Creek. Just watch for rocks, ruts, soft spots, and driveways.

10.4 Complete loop back where you started.

Gold Hill North

Location: Just east of Contest Point on Bottle Bay Road, south of Sandpoint, Idaho.

Distance: 11.5-mile loop.

Time: 80–120 minutes.

Tread: 8.4 miles singletrack, 3.1 miles forest road.

Aerobic level: Strenuous.

Technical difficulty: 2–4 on singletrack.

Hazards: Watch for hikers, horses, and wanderers seemingly from the 1960s. The usual 3Rs (rocks, roots, and ruts), steep switchbacks, flagellating berry vines, and punji stumps are also present. This trail is for experienced mountain bikers only.

Highlights: All of the items that are hazards also make this trail one of the finest, most pure and elegant mountain bike trails I've ever been on. The difficulty is sustained and technical but not impossible. It's a real climb but never a grunt, and it's predominantly singletrack, almost completely in the forest. This is a ride to work at and to perfect, for most. It can also be connected to larger loops coming down Forest Road 2642 through Garfield or Green Bay.

Land status: Idaho Panhandle National Forest/administered land.

Maps: Idaho Panhandle National Forest Travel Map; USGS Sandpoint, Idaho.

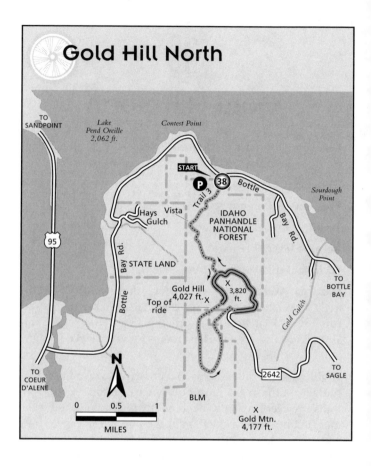

Gold Hill North

TO SANDPOINT

Lake Pend Oreille 2,062 ft.

Contest Point

START

P ③⑧ Bottle

Sourdough Point

Trail 3

Hays Gulch

Vista

IDAHO PANHANDLE NATIONAL FOREST

Bay Rd.

95

Bay Rd.

STATE LAND

Bottle

Gold Hill 4,027 ft. X

X 3,820 ft.

Top of ride

TO BOTTLE BAY

Gold Gulch

2642

TO SAGLE

TO COEUR D'ALENE

N

BLM

X Gold Mtn. 4,177 ft.

0   0.5   1

MILES

Access: Four miles south of Sandpoint, Idaho, on U.S. Highway 95, go east on Bottle Bay Road (paved). Follow the road 4.5 miles to Trail 3 trailhead. (If you're new to the area, make sure you bear left after crossing the railroad tracks.) There's limited parking at the trailhead (four or five cars, max), so be sure to park smart. The ride starts and ends here.

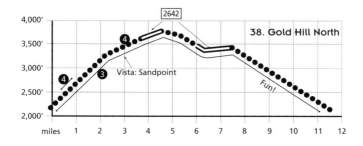

The Ride

0.0 From the Trail 3 trailhead pedal up a moderate grade (for the first 4 miles) on dirt singletrack. Cedars, hemlocks, and firs envelop you in a full canopy. The trail is mostly 2 feet wide and smooth dirt with occasional to frequent obstacles, mostly sustaining a 3 range of difficulty. After 50 yards, a 4 switchback greets you. Elevation 2,220 feet.

0.6 Glide.

0.7, 0.8 Two 4- switchbacks.

1.0 A 4 switchback, rocky. Then pass through a small clearing.

1.3 Grade lets up briefly as you cruise through a flat.

1.4 Rocky (3+).

1.6 Glide.

1.7 Climb through a series of three switchbacks.

2.1–2.2 Rocky (3+ to 4-).

2.4 Climb out of a wet area and through a rocky sidehill cut.

3.1+ Come to a rocky vista looking north over Sandpoint at 3,260 feet.

3.3- Climb through a tricky (4) section of loose and fixed rock.

3.5 Drop slightly for brief glide.

3.9 Climb up to FR 2642. Go right onto the forest road, climbing gently. It's wide with a mostly smooth, rock base. Elevation 3,610 feet.

4.4 Glide in to road's end. Continue on singletrack that picks up from here, diving back into trees. Elevation 3,710 feet.

4.5 Cruise smooth dirt.

4.7 Trail gets really fun through a section of rollers.

5.0 Come out of trees to a rocky prominence facing southeast. Follow the rocky and thin trail here as it makes a sharp right and descends. At 3,750 feet, you are at the summit of this ride and near the top of Gold Hill. Prepare yourself for the next mile—a roller-coaster ride: banked switchbacks, smooth surfaces, and good visibility.

5.3–5.5 Switchbacks.

6.0 Go left at FR 2642. Elevation 3,500 feet. Descend and cruise.

6.3 Bottom out at rock cuts. Elevation 3,430 feet. Then climb steeply.

6.4 Crest and glide.

6.5–6.9 Climb and dip with numerous crests.

7.1 Negotiate S turns.

7.2+ Just off road to right, there's a great vista of the lake.

7.6+ Go right off forest road back down onto Trail 3 the way you came. On the way out, you climbed almost 1,500 feet up this section. Going down is fun but technical, and watch out for all that ascending foot traffic.

11.5 Complete loop back at trailhead. If there's not a smile on your face, consider another sport.

Schweitzer Mountain

Location: 11 miles north of Sandpoint, Idaho.

Distance: 7.9 miles.

Time: 60–90 minutes.

Tread: 7 miles ski road/doubletrack; 0.9 mile singletrack.

Aerobic level: Moderate.

Technical difficulty: 3.

Hazards: This climb to the top of Schweitzer is the closest thing to a grunt in this book; it's steep and littered with rocks. Although it's mostly road, the surface serves up a lot of 3 (moderately difficult). Full suspension is suggested, but a front shock (at least) is highly recommended.

Highlights: The views of Lake Pend Oreille are classic postcard/ski magazine cover shots. The ski area road is the fastest, highest access to the southern Selkirks. This ride will give you a workout and introduce you to the Nordic trails and fun singletrack found in the lower eastern reaches of this area. There's a great singletrack, Nature Trail, that also leads to the top, but in the wisdom of the ski area, bikes are off-limits on that trail. There's also a full-service hotel/restaurant that's open through the summer. The high-speed quad lift to the top (at this time) runs Friday, Saturday, and Sunday, and it will take bikes during the summer from mid-June through Labor Day. It's best to call ahead to make sure the quad is running.

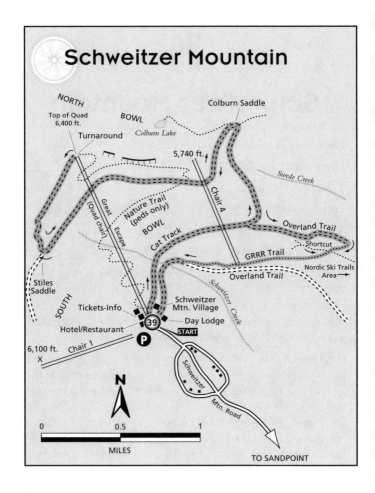

Land status: Schweitzer Mountain Resort land, privately owned but open to the public.

Maps: Schweitzer summer trail map; USGS Sandpoint, Idaho; Idaho Panhandle National Forest Travel Map (Sandpoint Ranger District).

Access: From Sandpoint, Idaho, go east on Idaho Highway 2 (north on 95). About a mile out of town, go left at the traffic light (north on 95). About 1.5 miles north, go left (west) on the Schweitzer Cut-Off Road (marked by signs to the ski area). Then follow the signs onto North Boyer right and off North Boyer left. This will lead you across railroad tracks to the Schweitzer Mountain Road, which leads to the ski hill itself. There's a big parking lot at the end, right in front of the mountain village. The ride begins and ends at the plaza in the center of the village.

The Ride

0.0 From the Schweitzer Mountain village plaza center, pedal north toward the base of the Great Escape quad chairlift. It's a mostly level gravel road. Elevation 4,700 feet.

0.1+ Pass quad chair to your left and Nordic trails entrance to your right. Then climb up a service road (the Cat Track) that is initially steep and rocky. Hint: If this first steep and bumpy section is a challenge for you, you may want to consider doing one of the more benign loops in the Nordic trail system, such as the Overland Trail or the GRRR (as in the

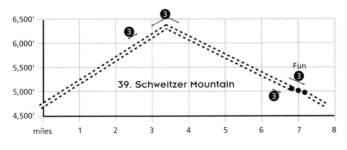

sound a tiger makes) Trail; they're described on Schweitzer's summer trail map.

0.3 Grade eases.

0.5 Pass under Chair 4.

0.8 Stay left to main Cat Track; Overland Trail goes right here.

1.6+ Go up and left here at the Colburn Saddle. Signs point the way (right) to Colburn Lake from here. Follow signs to Off the Top (on weekends, down-hillers will be screaming down this route, so watch out). Grade eases.

2.3 Grade goes steep, rocky (3).

3.1 Go right at Stiles Saddle. Climb steep, rocky, and winding road (3+).

3.4 Arrive at top of quad (6,400 feet); there are potties and drinking water (usually) here. After a good look over three mountain ranges and into Canada, go back down the way you came. Follow OFF THE TOP signs.

6.0 Go left off the Cat Track and onto Overland Loop Trail; smooth and flat.

6.1 Climb a short hill through S turns; pass Bone Yard (scrap, machinery) to your left.

6.2 At Y stay right to Overland Trail.

6.4 Drop through S turns (smooth, 3), passing single-track going off left.

6.7 Go right onto singletrack where Overland Trail goes left. Go left as singletrack splits into a rolling, fun section. Go left again where singletrack splits right.

6.8 Merge right and onto the GRRR Trail, which descends at a 3+ rate.

7.0 Cross creek through a lush section of swooping trail (3–4)!

7.1 Traverse sidehill through clearing (Abracadabra ski run) and then up quick bumps into cedars and shade (4-). Fun technical section follows.

7.5 Cross under Chair 4, descending rocky 3.

7.6 Merge right with Overland Trail, which is a level doubletrack here.

7.9 Complete loop back at village plaza.

Farther Afield

Columbia Mountain at Sherman Pass

Location: Sherman Pass, where Washington Highway 20 crosses the Kettle River Range.

Distance: 9.2 miles out and back with a loop.

Time: 70–90 minutes.

Tread: 0.4 mile forest road, 8.8 miles singletrack.

Aerobic level: Moderate.

Technical difficulty: 3+.

Hazards: Fixed rock, mostly, and some loose rock characterize this ride, with the exception of the start and finish. Full-sprung bikes were made for this kind of trail; otherwise, bring your hemorrhoid cream. Some exposure in spots; not sheer drop-offs. Hikers, bikers, and horses—and

Columbia Mountain at Sherman Pass

Trail 13 → To North Kettle Crest

Trail 16

To 2030

Trail 13

X Jungle Hill
6,500 ft.

6,720 ft.
X

Summit of ride
6,480 ft.

Trail 24

Columbia Mtn.
6,782 ft.
X

Spring

Trail 24

KETTLE

COLVILLE

NATIONAL

Trail 13

FOREST

Equestrian/Main
trailhead parking

Trail 82

20

TO
KETTLE
FALLS

Pass Creek

Sherman Pass
Campground

Trail 82

Trail 96

START

20

Sherman
Pass
5,587 ft.

Trail 13

40

Nature
trail

Drinking
water

CREST

N

To Snow Peak

Sherman Peak
X   6,998 ft.

0   0.5   1

MILES

watch the highway! This is a strong intermediate-to-advanced ride.

Highlights: This is just a small sample of the high-quality subalpine singletrack trails found at Kettle Crest. The crest itself is a spine of more than a dozen peaks running north-south from Sherman Pass to a hut 15 miles north (check the Kettle Falls Ranger District for reservations). The trails connecting the pass and the hut are a legacy of old cattle drives, packsaddles, and engineless times. What remains is excellent singletrack! Kettle Crest trails are closed to motorized travel.

Land status: Colville National Forest.

Maps: Colville National Forest Visitors Map; USGS Sherman Peak, Washington.

Access: From Spokane, travel 75 minutes north to Colville on U.S. Highway 395. Bunny hop through Kettle Falls (the ranger district office is located here), across the Columbia River, and then left (west) on WA 20. About 20 miles up is Sherman Pass Campground to the right (north); there'll also be a SCENIC TRAIL sign. Parking is limited in the campground, so if you drive west on the highway a bit farther, you'll see signs for the official trailhead and parking to the right. The ride starts and ends at the campground road just off the highway.

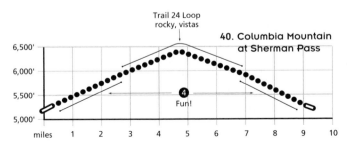

The Ride

0.0 Pedal into campground road, sandy and smooth. Just into the trees, go left at the T, following signs to Trail 96. Elevation 5,200 feet.

0.1 Bear left where campground loop road splits. It's cool and shady here.

0.2 Go right onto Trail 96. There's a hand pump for drinking water from a well just before and to the left. The trailhead sign is faint, and the start of the trail is subtle, but once you get onto it, it's like Disneyland, a 4-foot-wide, gray gravel snake (2).

0.5 Cross over a series of five wooden bridges, some with rails.

0.6 One more bridge, then up a quick switchback right. Here the gravel cattle highway ends and dirt single-track climbs through thick undergrowth (3).

0.7+ Go left and up a gentler grade, wider track (2+). This is Trail 82.

0.9+ Trail gets bumpier and steeper (4-).

1.0+ Come to a T; this is where Trail 82 meets Trail 13 (Kettle Crest Trail). Go up and right, along Trail 13, on steeper, rutted uphill (4-).

1.1- Cross trailhead road (gravel) and continue up Trail 13, steep.

1.2 Sign in at trail register box on your right. Tread goes to mixed granite-dirt (a recurring theme), and grade eases to moderate-steep (3-).

1.3–2.5 Climb through a series of short, steep, rocky pitches. A couple of easier glides at the top end of this section are rewards for your perseverance. Sustained 4 range of difficulty with an occasional 5 for humility.

2.5 Glide and climb gentle sidehill through aspens and wildflowers (2+). Elevation 5,860 feet.

2.7 Cruise excellent contour line with fun obstacles (3-). Views over WA 20, Sherman Peak. Elevation 5,920 feet.

3.4+ Go right onto Columbia Mountain Trail 24, marked by a sign. Trail 13 continues off left. Climb moderate sidehill with great views. Elevation 6,030 feet.

3.5 Pass spring and Lookout Camp (marked under big fir) to your left.

4.0 Trail 24 splits into loop. Go sharp left, along 2-foot-high rock wall. Elevation 6,360 feet. Granite buttresses directly above guard the summit of Columbia Mountain. Rocky-dirt trail on this loop section (to mile 5.4) is mostly in the 3 range.

4.3 Climb and crest, and dip through meadow to a steep 4.

4.4 Summit this ride (6,480 feet) in rocky saddle. To left (west) is rocky crag, and to right is thin singletrack (best to leave bike) that threads up steeply through undergrowth to summit of Columbia Mountain (grab your map and check out the crest). Drop steeply a short bit on rocky, winding trail.

4.5+ Talus field, then come around corner to vistas north and east.

4.8 Trail eases a bit (2+), then rolls, dips, and climbs.

5.4 Meet back at where you entered this loop. Go left and down.

6.2 Go sharp left and back down Trail 13.

6.8 Climb short 4, rocky.

7.0–7.8 Switchbacks, rocky (4-).

7.9 Swoop through a sustained "grotto" of bouldery turns (4)!

8.1 Trail eases, gets a bit wider (3-).

8.2 Sign out at trail box, and then cross trailhead road.

8.2+ Make a sharp left onto Trail 96/82.

8.5 Go right onto narrow, brushy Hiker Trail (signed) and down.

8.6 Trail widens to gravel wonderland, crossing bridges.

9.0 Enter campground, following road back left, then right to complete this classic ride at 9.2 miles.

Appendix A

Other Spokane-Area Routes

Here's a short listing, with brief descriptions and directions, of other areas to ride within a couple hours of the Spokane–Coeur d'Alene area. For the most part, these areas are higher in elevation and are more suitable for summer and fair-weather conditions.

Batey-Bould ORV Area: An hour and a half north of Spokane, between Chewelah and Newport, you'll find this fun trail system. The best access is west off of Washington Highway 20 north of Newport, onto Kapps or West Calispell Roads to the main trailhead. Although this system was principally designed for motorized vehicles, who use it well, it offers some great surprises: Pend Oreille River Valley views and an old preserved homestead, just to name a couple. Numerous stream crossings, loops around Tacoma Peak and Boulder Mountain, and connections to the Little Pend Oreille Trail System characterize this area. Just remember, this is a shared-use area, and weekends may be busy. It's part of the Colville National Forest; look for information in Colville or Newport on this area.

Kettle Crest Trail: From Spokane take U.S. Highway 395 north to Colville (one hour), then go west on Washington Highway 20, passing through Kettle Falls and over Roosevelt Lake, and climbing to Sherman Pass (elevation 5,575 feet). This is the easiest access point for this amazing area. Great singletrack follows the ridge of the Kettle River Range, which stretches north-south almost to Canada. From Snow Peak and Sherman Peak just south of the pass to a ridge connecting more than a dozen peaks leading to Mount Leona to the north, you have the option of riding Trail 13 (singletrack) or Forest Road 380 (easier, but heavily traveled). These two routes parallel the ridge and are connected by Trails 15, 16, and 75, allowing for many options on this 70-plus-mile loop system. Ryan Cabin is between Mount Leona and Profanity Peak; you can check out availability at the district ranger station in Kettle Falls. The Sherman Pass Recreation Area also offers limited camping, drinking water, and a picnic area.

Little Pend Oreille River and Lakes Area: About an hour and half north of Spokane, go through Colville via U.S. Highway 395 and then east on Washington Highway 20 to some of the most scenic forested wetlands in the entire region. A string of lakes are connected by WA 20 and the Little Pend Oreille (pronounced Pond aRAY) River. Colville National Forest campgrounds at Leo, Thomas, and Gillette Lakes offer a range of amenities; trails are abundant north, east, and west of here. Little Twin Lakes and the Little Pend Oreille Wildlife Recreation Area just southwest offer a whole other range of trails. Granite Peak and McDonald Mountain can be considered two good options at either end of this section of the Selkirk Mountains.

Lookout Pass: This is a significant geologic and geographic place. Not only is this the juncture of the Bitterroot, St. Joe, and Coeur d'Alene mountain ranges, it's the administrative juncture of three national forests. Aside from the easy access that Lookout Pass Ski Area provides, old railroad grades and packsaddle trails lead to subalpine lakes, high passes, and mines. Use caution whenever in mining country (some mines are still operational), and note that some trails are steep and rocky. Generally, the area immediately south of the pass is less disturbed. The area between Stevens Peak and Lookout Pass offers a number of subalpine lakes accessed by singletrack. It's located on the Idaho-Montana border about an hour east of Coeur d'Alene via I–90. Elevations range between 4,000 and 7,000 feet.

North Fork of the Coeur d'Alene River: A half hour east of Coeur d'Alene on I–90 take exit 43 at Kingston, following North Fork Road north through Enaville. Go another 40 to 50 minutes to the Avery Creek Campground. From there you can park and pedal to a couple of fun rides; one is up North Fork Road another 2 miles. Turn right at Forest Road 442 and right again onto Trails 502 or 153 (both singletrack), which loop back to FR 442 at Taylor Saddle for a 20-miler. Another ride is up North Fork Road another half hour to near the end of the pavement; climb right, up Trail 208 past Steamboat Rock and Cathedral Rocks. You connect with FR 403 left to Trail 3099 and then left down singletrack Trail 309 to loop back just upstream on Teepee Creek near where you went in. Or, cut across FR 403 and proceed to the Coeur d'Alene National Recreation Trail. The North Fork of the Coeur d'Alene is a huge area, and time spent exploring will bear fruit.

Trail of the Coeur d'Alenes: This recent rail-to-trail project stretches from Plummer to Mullan, Idaho, covering a distance of almost 70 miles. Its overall grade is less than 1 percent, which means its slight ups and downs are hardly noticeable. As of early 2003 it was still under construction by the Union Pacific Railroad, which owns and has operated this line for almost a century. Once the swing bridge over Lake Coeur d'Alene is raised and work on the final section between Plummer and the bridge is completed, it will offer one of the most scenic and pleasurable rail trails in the country. This continuous ribbon of asphalt will be a huge attraction not only to bikers (both roadies and rutters) but also to skaters, joggers, walkers, and strollers. The nonmotorized pathway will boast rest rooms, picnic facilities, and signboards pointing out historic and natural features. One feature of the trail is that it follows or crosses water over almost its entire course, traversing Lake Coeur d'Alene's southern end (which itself harbors lakes within the larger lake), the St. Joe River (a river within a lake), and the Coeur d'Alene River (which forms an entire chain of lakes stretching over 20 miles). You can access this wonderful cooperative effort (thanks to Union Pacific, the Coeur d'Alene Tribe, and Idaho State Parks and Recreation) from a number of locations; here are a few: Plummer (just west of US 95 or just east off Highway 5); Heyburn State Park (on Highway 5 also, 7 miles east of Plummer); Harrison (Highway 97 on the east side of Lake Coeur d'Alene); Old Mission State Park (near Cataldo on Interstate 90); or at Kellogg, Wallace, or Mullan (all on I–90).

Appendix B

Information Sources

Friends of the Centennial Trail
P.O. Box 351
Spokane, WA 99201-0351
(509) 624-7188

Instrumental in galvanizing public support for the Centennial Trail (a model dedicated pedestrian/nonmotorized pathway following the Spokane River), this group's purpose is to assist and encourage development and maintenance of the Spokane River Centennial Trail, adjacent state park development, and connecting trails.

Spokane Mountaineers
P.O. Box 1013
Spokane, WA 99201
(509) 838-4974 (voice mail)

Not connected to the Seattle Mountaineers, this group represents climbers, hikers, and bikers who love and frequent the mountains of the Inland Northwest. They have good information on trails, access points, and issues concerning recreational uses of our uplands. If you're new to the area, consider joining; it's a great way to get acquainted with the region's offerings.

Spokane Bicycle Club
P.O. Box 62
Spokane, WA 99201
(509) 325-1171

Mostly representing road riders, this club is active in local bike issues. Their committed membership strives to make bike riding a lifestyle, not just a sport. In good weather they ride weekly, and bikers of all persuasions are invited.

Taft Tunnel Preservation Society
(208) 556-1523 or (208) 744-1392
This group maintains and manages the Hiawatha Rail Trail in cooperation with Idaho Panhandle National Forest.

Parks

Coeur d'Alene Parks Department
221 South Fifth Street
Coeur d'Alene, ID 83814
(208) 769-2252

Farragut State Park
13400 East Ranger Road
Athol, ID 83801
(208) 683-2425

Heyburn State Park
1291 Chatcolet Road
Plummer, ID 83851
(208) 686-1308

Liberty Lake County Park
3707 South Zephyr Road
Liberty Lake, WA 99019
(509) 255-6861

Mount Spokane State Park
26107 North Mount Spokane
    Drive
Mead, WA 99021
(509) 456-4169, 238-6845

Riverside State Park
4427 North Aubrey White
    Parkway
Spokane, WA 99205-3995
(509) 456-3964

Spokane City Parks and Recreation
808 West Spokane Falls Boulevard
Spokane, WA 99201
(509) 625-6200

Spokane County Parks and Recreation
404 North Havana
Spokane, WA 99212
(509) 456-4730

Bureau of Land Management

Spokane District Office
1103 North Fancher
Spokane, WA 99212-1275
(509) 536–1200

National Forests

Colville National Forest Offices

Supervisor's Office
Federal Building
765 South Main
Colville, WA 99114
(509) 684–3711

Kettle Falls Ranger District
255 West 11th Street
Kettle Falls, WA 99141
(509) 738–6111

Newport Ranger District
315 North Warren
Newport, WA 99156
(509) 447–3129

Idaho Panhandle National Forest Offices

Avery Office, St. Joe Ranger District
HC Box 1
Avery, ID 83802
(208) 245–4517

Fernan Ranger District
2502 East Sherman
Coeur d'Alene, ID 83814
(208) 769–3038

Sandpoint Ranger District
1500 Highway 2
Sandpoint, ID 83864
(208) 263–5111

An Index of Rides

Glossary

ATB: All-terrain bicycle; aka mountain bike, sprocket rocket, fat-tire flyer.

ATV: All-terrain vehicle; in this book *ATV* refers to motorbikes and three- and four-wheelers designed for off-road use.

Bail: Getting off the bike, usually in a hurry, and whether or not you meant to. Often a last resort.

Bollard: A vertical post at a trailhead, like a stile, usually used to restrict motor vehicles.

Bunny hop: Leaping up, while riding, and lifting both wheels off the ground to jump over an obstacle (or for sheer joy).

Clean: To ride without touching a foot (or other body part) to the ground; to ride a tough section successfully.

Clipless: A type of pedal with a binding that accepts a special cleat on the soles of bike shoes. The cleat clicks in for more control and efficient pedaling, and out for safe landings (in theory).

Contour: A line on a topographic map showing a continuous elevation level over uneven ground. Also used as a verb to indicate a fairly easy or moderate grade: "The trail contours around the canyon rim before the final grunt to the top."

Dab: To put a foot or hand down (or hold onto or lean on a tree or other support) while riding. If you have to dab, then you haven't ridden that piece of trail clean.

Downfall: Trees that have fallen across the trail.

Doubletrack: A trail, jeep road, ATV route, or other track with two distinct ribbons of tread, typically with grass growing in between. No matter which side you choose, the other rut always looks smoother.

Draw: A depression or swale on the topography, usually without steep sides.

Endo: Lifting the rear wheel off the ground and riding (or abruptly not riding) on the front wheel only. Also known, at various degrees of control and finality, as a nose wheelie, "going over the handlebars," and a face plant.

Exposed: A section of trail that exposes you to the danger of going off the trail, usually with serious physical injury as a result. Unsure riders should get off and walk their bikes.

Fall line: The angle and direction of a slope; the line you follow when gravity is in control and you aren't.

Graded: When a gravel road is scraped level to smooth out the washboards and potholes, it has been graded. In this book, a road is listed as graded only if it is regularly maintained. Not all such roads are graded every year, however.

Granny gear: The lowest (easiest) gear, a combination of the smallest of the three chain rings on the bottom bracket spindle (where the pedals and crank arms attach to the bike's frame) and the largest cog on the rear cluster. Shift down to your granny gear for serious climbing.

Grunt: A difficult ride or section of a ride, usually uphill, steep, and sustained.

Hammer: To ride hard; derived from how it feels afterward: "I'm hammered."

Kelly hump: An abrupt mound of dirt across the road or trail. These are common on old logging roads and skidder tracks, placed there to block vehicle access. At high speeds, they become launching pads for bikes and inadvertent astronauts.

Line: The route (or trajectory) between or over obstacles or through turns. *Tread* or *trail* refers to the ground you're riding on; the line is the path you choose within the tread (and exists mostly in the eye of the beholder).

Off-the-seat: Moving your butt behind the bike seat and over the rear tire; used for control on extremely steep descents. This position increases braking power, helps prevent endos, and reduces skidding.

Portage: To carry the bike, usually up a steep hill, across unridable obstacles or through a stream.

Punji stake/stump: Any sharp, nasty, pointy stake or stick projecting out of the ground. They present the opportunity for serious bodily injury. In north Idaho, they are usually the stumps of small trees not cut off at ground level.

Quads: Thigh muscles (short for quadriceps) or maps in the USGS topographic series (short for quadrangles).

Ratcheting: Also known as backpedaling; pedaling backward to avoid hitting rocks or other obstacles with the pedals.

Roller: A rolling, undulating section of trail.

Scree: Medium-to-small-size rock debris.

Sidehill: Where the trail crosses a slope. If the tread is narrow, keep your inside (uphill) pedal up to avoid hitting the ground. If the tread tilts downhill, you may have to use some body language to keep the bike plumb or vertical to avoid slipping out.

Singletrack: A trail, game run, or other track with only one ribbon of tread. Good singletrack is pure fun.

Spur: A side road or trail that splits off from the main route.

Surf: Riding through loose gravel or sand, when the wheels sway from side to side. Also heavy surf: frequent and difficult obstacles.

Suspension: A bike with front suspension has a shock-absorbing fork or stem. Rear suspension absorbs shock between the rear wheel and frame. A bike with both is said to be fully suspended.

Switchbacks: When a trail goes up a steep slope, it zigzags or switchbacks across the fall line to ease the gradient of the climb. Well-designed switchbacks make a turn with at least an 8-foot radius and remain fairly level within the turn itself. These are rare, however, and cyclists often struggle to ride through sharply angled, sloping switchbacks.

Talus: Larger-size rock debris (cantaloupe and larger).

Topo: Topographic map, showing elevation contour lines.

Tread: The riding surface, particularly regarding single-track.

Treewell: A hole in the earth left by a fallen tree.

Trials: A specialized form of mountain bike competition that exhibits stunt and extreme obstacle-handling skills.

Water bar: A log, rock, or other barrier placed in the tread to divert water off the trail and prevent erosion. Peeled logs can be slippery and cause bad falls, especially when they angle sharply across the trail.

Whoop-dee-doo: A series of kelly humps used to keep vehicles off trails. Watch your speed or do the dreaded top tube tango.

Winder: A winding, usually fun section of trail.

About the Author

Martin Potucek has lived in Idaho since 1972, climbing, skiing, and eventually biking in some of its most pristine parts, with Spokane never far away. He has gone from building homes in Sandpoint to teaching English at the University of Idaho and Washington State University in the Palouse to technical and recreational writing in Boise. He and his family now base out of Spokane but hover in Idaho.

FALCON GUIDES®

From nature exploration to extreme adventure, FalconGuides lead you there. With more than 400 titles available, there is a guide for every outdoor activity and topic, including essential outdoor skills, field identification, trails, trips, and the best places to go in each state and region. Written by experts, each guidebook features detailed descriptions, maps, and advice that can enhance every outdoor experience.

You can count on FalconGuides to lead you to your favorite outdoor activities wherever you live or travel.

MOUNTAIN BIKING

These local mountain biking guides comprehensively cover the best local riding in a region, usually around an urban area. They are small, lightweight, and fit nicely into a bike jersey pocket.

4 ¼" x 7" · paperback · maps, elevation graphs

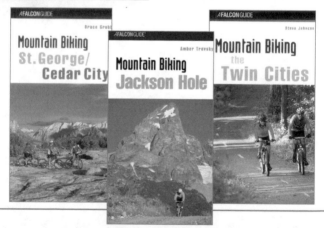

For a complete selection of titles on outdoor recreation, travel, and history, check with your local bookseller or visit us on-line at www.globe-pequot.com and www.falcon.com.